WiLLARD & MAPLE XV

Literary and fine arts magazine of Champlain College

ACKNOWLEDGEMENTS

EDITOR-IN-CHIEF   Alyssa Stearns
PRODUCTIONS EDITOR   Nicholas Walge
LAYOUT & DESIGN EDITOR Morgaine Jennings
COVER DESIGN   Nick Stefani
COVER PHOTOGRAPHY   Derek Johnson,
                      (*Winner of the Willard & Maple Art Award*)

ASSOCIATE EDITORS:

Josh Adler	Patience Hulburt-Lawton
Katherine Brockway	Ryan Leung
Anthony Carace	Cassie McHarris
Abigail Clark	Will Ryan
Ryan Egan	Stephanie Schmidt
Craig Ellsworth	Philip Smith
Erin Gleeson	Alexander Spera
Cassie Guerrera	Carissa Stimpfel
Matthew Henebury	Claire Weaver
Christy Jennett	Sarah Wheeler
	Jordan Zehr

{5}

CONTENTS

{6}

Literary and Fine Art Magazine of Champlain Colege

LETTER FROM THE EDITOR
Alyssa Stearns

Dear Readers and Contributors,

Season's Greetings! Thank you all for your patience and passion for the art captured within this issue of Willard & Maple. My first full year as editor-in-chief of Champlain College's literary and art magazine has been rife with challenge and splendor. The 2009 to 2010 school year has forged and tested friendships, challenged my identity as a student and role model, and made me wiser (I think).

After a refreshing summer, and with issue XIV still incomplete, Nick Walge sauntered into Jim Ellefson's office, (the workspace used by Willard & Maple) and became my co-editor. Nick was already a friend of mine, but that did not mean we knew how to work together. Learning how to communicate my ideas and needs to another person and effectively delegate responsibilities were my major challenges this time around. I realized that I'm not the best teacher, and that I have trouble letting go of my control over situations. Thankfully, every Thursday, Nick and I were able to blow off some steam in class with the Editorial Board, most of whom were at a similar point in their college careers (seniors, that is). In this fun, productive setting, we could let loose and take on almost an entertainer role, as well as facilitate some insightful conversation about the work presented.

Nick and I threw a winter fundraiser, which came together beautifully but was poorly attended. Still, the stylish presentation of the visual art and the quality of the musical performances assured me that when I tried it again, it would only be an improvement.

Second semester, I moved on without Nick's help. It was sort of a rude awakening, the first class I held without that banter. Having no one else there to help with the often mundane, routine office tasks also proved to be somewhat of a drag. The Editorial Board was different, too; most were what I considered "hard to please" at the time. Willard & Maple XV, as a result, is the slim product of selective acceptance, which truly is a change I've wanted to see since my editorship began. Although it was hard sometimes to see pieces I loved getting tossed aside, I suppose I got what I asked for—an increase in the quality of the magazine, and I believe that's what we have here.

I tried to bring similar scrutiny to our spring fundraiser. The "Ice-Out Art Shout" was intended to be a celebration of the winter passing and of us as a community moving on to a more colorful, splendid, creative future. I posted beautiful fliers all over Burlington (designed by Champlain alumn Michael Fagan), pestered every friend I had for connections to local bands, and recruited some folks from a bi-monthly poetry reading in town.

Combined with our own poetic community from Champlain, our reading was overflowing with talent! We had to worry about running out of time before running out of poets, which had never before been a concern of mine, even at readings I did not organize. It was more challenging this time around to find artists, but some very talented painters and photographers contributed, and their work looked amazing. We also had a diverse collection of local bands, ranging from keyboard-based jazz-rock trio, Healthy Option Dane; blues-rock band The Nose; harmonica-heavy blues, with a great offering of unexpected covers by The Holy Devils; bass-heavy, rude and scintillating rock by the Feverbreakers; and wrapped up the evening with two-guys-and-a-girl original hip-hop by the Lynguistic Civilians, who have since been performing all over town.

Willard & Maple has seen me through some challenging times, and I hope it stands as a beacon of purpose for some of you as well. Sometimes, sitting in the office reading all your wonderful submissions and

answering your questions was the only solace I could take from haunting
thoughts about the futility of higher education. As a senior, I became
disillusioned and distrustful of the system all college students and
faculty are a part of. But let Willard & Maple be a symbol of truth in
a world steeped in lies. It is you, it is me; it's our whole experience
bound by one spine.

I want to send out special thanks to Nick Walge, who brought unend-
ing positivity and cordiality to the Willard & Maple office, as well
as stunning eloquence and good humor. Also, thanks to all the bands,
artists, and poets who shared their talents with us during the last two
fundraisers. All of you, as well as all of the independent donors, raised
over $800 in the past year. I have no doubt in my mind that our wonderful
little magazine can expand and flourish for years to come.

I am forever indebted to Morgaine Jennings and Nick Stefani, first
of all, for their expertise in visual art and layout, and secondly, for
their patience.

Thanks to all the Associate Editors who showed up each week and
dealt with distractions, disagreements, and a marked lack of snacks dur-
ing our board meetings.

It's been a milestone year here, and it continues to be a fight to
stay above water. But I hope this issue makes a remarkable imprint on
the lives of your friends, family, colleagues, lovers, enemies, and
especially the strangers that see themselves reflected in the words of a
little-known poet in print. May our community continue to grow!

Thank you again, and I send the best of the best wishes to you all.

Sincerely,
Alyssa Stearns

LETTER FROM THE EDITOR
Nick Wagle

When I first met with J. C. Ellefson–poet-in-residence to Champlain, honorary big brother to his students, and faculty advisor to the Willard and Maple–to discuss my position on the editorial staff of the literary magazine, we were both rolling our eyes to some degree. We had to do some paperwork to satisfy some program requirements, and the task seemed a little tedious, but obligatory. But as is often the case with Jim, the conversation that we feared would be forced turned into something much more substantive. The answer we formed when it came time to fill in the three lines provided on the Student Internship Form under the question "What will be the student's role for this internship?" still sticks out to me: "Be the literary conduit that links an author to his or her audience."

In hindsight, the phrasing seems a tad boisterous; the conduit was much larger than my two arms spread wide. But being a part of that chain, holding onto the string that links the paper cup in Ohio to the book that you now hold in your hands, has been a nonetheless exhilarating experience.

I can recall the anticipation every time I held a sealed manila envelope in my hand, wondering if this would be the piece that we at the Willard and Maple were waiting for. I can still imagine the individual authors in my mind's eye, my imagination constructing a work place for each and everyone as I read their work. I can still feel the sense of satisfaction after reading the part that our contributor just absolutely nailed, or the awe of stumbling upon a completely unique idea.

I remember meeting with our editorial board, and marveling at how many different things could be taken away from a piece that I had not noticed before, or fighting for a piece that I felt deserved another shot.

This volume of the Willard and Maple is the final product of the creativity of our contributors, the direction of our staff, and the support of our audience, and I hope you enjoy it.

I would like to first thank our contributors, both past and present. Not only do your submissions make our magazine possible, but they inspire our entire staff.

I would also like to thank the entire Willard and Maple staff for their contributions this year, with a very special thanks to Alyssa Stearns, without whom this issue would not have been possible.

Finally, I would like to thank our readers, and here's to hoping that the Willard and Maple will be continue to be a source of inspiration for you as it has been for me.

Nick Walge

LITERARY ARTS

Literary and Fine Art Magazine of Champlain College

AcE BOGGESS

"What Kind of Plastic Surgery Would I Ask for My Soul?"

First the scars. Mostly the scars.
Streaks of white & red across the Invisible.
With precision tools
somewhere between laser scalpel &
deus ex machina,
I'd have them cut away,
erased, replaced with tattoos
of circus clowns
or a prairie fire
that wipes the landscape clean.
Nip here, tuck there,
injections to brighten &
clarify. Or, maybe I
should enhance instead,
add some needed character
to that unseen part of me.
I could make new scars
that swear ugliness is beautiful,
could cloak myself in them
from thought to DNA
until I leave my chrysalis
a man made up of only scars:
pastiche, collage,
a burned omelet of scars.
Otherwise, nothing further
need be done.
No change at all.

{13}

ACE BOGGESS

"What Are Reason and Sobriety
Without Knowledge of Intoxication?"

The folks in AA call them *Earth People,*
not to sketch them in caricature—
common, unthinking—but to show how alien we are
to those who've never taken the hard journey,
as if we've stepped off a star bus: mutants, terrible,
with Cubist eyes, red proboscises
from powders, gin blossoms, dried blood, *etc.*
Ours is the lost language of a race doomed
to hunt itself out of existence: our weapons
unknown to Everyman, or anyone
who never held a gun to his head &
laughed. Speak to an *Earth Man*
of addictions or "chasing the dragon,"
he'll say, "Just quit," or think about fairy tales
where the princess finds her prince &
all's well that ends, if perhaps a little dull.
But, that dragon exists, devours us from inside
like cancer without the sympathy,
a rotting of the soul. We suffer:
a dangerous bunch of astro-nots,
travelers going nowhere: *Earth Beings,*
take us to your leader. We do not come in peace.

{14}

ANDREW OERKE

City Park By Dark

This is a park pretending it's country.
A dead-serious silence threatens the grounds.
Shadows sell themselves to the dark side.
Cops patrol the edges of the grid
as regularly as farmers wheel the grind.

As punctually as Night unfolds its powers,
flowers tuck their petals under their wings
and the sepals close up, the poor things.
Stars n planets plant look-alikes in the towers.

{15}

As greensleeves stain in the throbbing grass,
blue boys double their skinny in pools without waves;
but no one dares do such things here at night
so love must happen in movies n toons
since there's only cement in all of these ruins.

ARTHUR GOTTLIEB

End of the Line

Puffing, a train pulls in
to the last terminal. Wings
of steam fly to the steel buttresses
supporting a space
huge as a medieval cathedral.

Gargoyles grab our baggage.
The engine breathes relief
as we stream into the waiting room.

Dust stains the windows.
A clock looms like a moon
whose hands, stuck at high noon,
cut off light like giant scissors.

We doze on benches hard as pews
waiting to be taken
from this depressing place
to the next station.

Thin ribs of rail
come down to meet us,
their ties forming a ladder
leading to the mouth of a tunnel,
which opens without a word
wide enough to receive us.

How many times
have you killed yourself
getting to a place
you never needed to be?

Realizing once you arrived
how the ridiculous gives
absurdity a sublime voice.

Even a bad name. Now,
your windup doll is winded
from running up too many bills.

And stares. Wish you could
get behind the wheel and drive
until the rearview mirror holds
nothing but distant memories
of yesterday's mistakes.

Picture the police
bent over a body, measuring
lengths and breaths to solve
the mystery of last week's
            hit and run.

Taking notes home to their teachers.
And suspicious wives.

After years of night, sunrise
surprises. After eating
the figments of our imaginationfrom the dishes of priests &
princes,

Inquisitors with identical dental
IDs sprinkle shredded documents
            over our just desserts.

Socks full of pulled punches
packed safely away in our drawers.
But in our playground a pyramid
of ribs ripped from cadavers
lacking caskets stacked in a ditch for dogs to scavenge.

Willard & Maple XV

{17}

BARRY W. NORTH

Alone

In a gray dawn,
standing
on the edge of the gulf,
as upon the edge of time,
watching the rain beat,
in elemental sensuality,
upon the immense breast of the open sea,
life,
as a spontaneous eruption,
without the touch of God,
seems almost conceivable,
with implications more frightening
than anything in The Bible.
Man, rooted not in the heavens
but in spongy river bottoms,
eventually rising to the trees,
before dropping,
club in hand,
to terrorize the open plains,
and multiplying into animals,
roaming city streets,
punching the eyes out of each of their victims,
like hoodlums smashing windows in a vacant house.

{18}

BARRY W. NORTH

Eleven

That day,
we followed the mid-city parade,
from beginning to end,
as it meandered down
the streets of New Orleans.
Like the little invaders we were,
we chased the floats
through block after block
of strange neighborhoods,
darting in and out of the crowd,
joyfully out-maneuvering

and out-jumping
the frustrated, stodgy adults
passively reaching up for the useless junk.

That night,
we lay on the back of the porch,
bone-weary,
like dogs after a hunt,
listening to my older brother,
and his teenage friends,
cast and re-cast
their new adult voices
out into the night air,
beneath the strains
of Earth Angel
playing on the radio
and the giggles of girls

posing as women
on the front steps,
while we,
masters of our universe,

lay in the dark,
silent as shadows,
staring out at the strange new world,
looming,
just beyond the edge of the planet.

{20}

BRIAN STEEN
Before the Street Lights Come On

I can't keep up, no way, no how. I am pedaling for my life and Russell has already rounded Sarasota and probably made it to Joy road already.

I like my 20 inch bike a lot, so don't get me wrong, but I'm not a 20 inch kid anymore, and all the kids are getting 26 inch Schwinn ten-speeds, with the hand brakes clamped to the ram's horn handlebars. I still like my coaster brake better 'cause I can kick back my left heel fast on the pedal and stop completely, which has to be better than those little pads of rubber on all those ten-speeds.

Only thing is, I don't like being behind, watching the ten-speed people pull away in their little groups of actin' superior, which means they think they're a bit more special than me.

I can't lie…I want a ten-speed, I do. But I'm not really tall enough for one yet, only Russell, who's my twin, but not identical, who just happens to be way taller than me. Nope, I'm not tall enough yet, only old enough, which doesn't count for nothing here, with this problem.

Russell, yeah Russell. He thinks he's a lot better than me now since he saved his paper route money and I spent my money on albums and 45's. But still, even if I had the money there'd be no sense at all to owning something you can't use right now, only later.

When I think about it too, I guess Russell has always been better at everything that really counts when you're almost twelve. Like with football; Russell can throw perfect spirals almost every time, and Russell gets to be quarterback almost always, while I'm never quarterback, not even once, unless nobody else is around in my neighborhood, and I'm only pretending.

And baseball, which is the season we're in now, well Russell can hit it farther than me, and he has a better arm, and he can always say "No way!" to playing outfield because it's infield all the way, or no way at all for Russell. I always get stuck out in left field where there's hardly ever any action, and so I start to daydream so when a ball is actually hit out to me, I'm always chasing after it.

Hockey is even worse. Who can skate on blades? The day we both got out of two blades and got genuine hockey skates was a day that should've been proud, but it wasn't. For me it was the day my ankles flopped over sideways and ever since I've been only trying to play hockey. But Russell's ankles, for some reason, are strong. He skates fast and looks tough and has that look he stole from the big hockey stars in the NHL that says he could fire a puck at your head at 90 miles per hour, no problem, and probably never even **{22}** blink, or feel bad about it. I can't pull that off. Russell always makes sure before we even get to the rink to announce: "When I get the puck Randy, you just better get out of the way unless you want that puck buried in your forehead!" So far I have no scars, only close calls all the times the puck has whizzed by my head. Our goalie though, Norm Mason, who has always played goalie for my side lots of winters, he got hit in the chest last winter by Russell's slap shot. As soon as it hit, Norm started bawling his eyes out, and Norm, he's real fat, almost 220 at twelve years! And Norm even had two jackets on and cardboard over his shins and chest, and a catcher's mask over his big face! Norm just slumped over when Russell's puck slammed into him, and then cried his fat face fuller. Next day though, Norm came prepared. This time the cardboard padding was gone and Norm had steel garbage can lids roped to his body.

But right now, here I am, in the summer, in my drive-way, on my 20 inch bike, feeling younger than I am because it seems like the whole neighborhood is gone. Russell got Eric and Patrick and Steve and Johnny and Ted and Tony to all go with him at 10:00 sharp this morning, to ride all the way up Telegraph Road to Tel-Twelve Mall. That's like ten miles one way! Now how am I supposed to keep up all that way with a one speed, small sprocket bike and not fall far behind quick? No way at all. When I watched Russell and all of my friends disappear 'round Sarasota this morning, it felt like going to a Detroit Tigers game on Hat Day and not getting a hat, or like going to the movies and being told you can't have any popcorn.

My Mom yells out the screen door: "What happened to all the boys? Where's Russell?" That's what it always is: "Where's Russell?" It's never "Where's Randy?" 'cause right now here's Randy, like always, behind.

"They said they were going for a long ride" I answer, and that's all, thinking that no way did Russell tell mom he was going all the way up Telegraph, ten miles up, and then ten miles back.

Mom opens the screen door now and cups her left hand over her eyebrows to keep the sun out. "A long ride where? He didn't say where he was going?" mom asks.

Now I'm really in a bind, since I figure none of us have ever been that far before, unsupervised, even though we do ten miles a day easily, just never in a straight line.

"I don't know, I just know he took everybody with him, so probably far, somewhere" is all I say.

"How far?" Mom needles, now actually coming out on the porch on this sticky Michigan summer day. But inside our house it's just as sticky, with just the fan taking in the breeze from outside and blowing it all over our living room. Some of my friends have air conditioners in their living rooms now, but not us and probably never.

"Maybe to the mall" I say, squirming some, figuring I'm done explaining and how I better leave now, pedal down to Norm's house, and besides, Norm has to be home 'cause he can't pedal anything.

"The mall? You mean Korvette's? Or did he go way out to Wonderland Mall? I hope not. He knows I don't want him going that far. There are just too many crazies out there!" Mom rambles, hopefully answering her own questions. Wonderland Mall isn't even that far, maybe five miles one way, tops. But it's a crappy mall, so who would want to go there, since it's old, and all outside, not like Tel-Twelve Mall, that's all enclosed and air-conditioned.

"I don't know, Mom" I lie, which is something I don't usually do, except when I have to, when it seems like a better idea than telling the truth. Like in early grade school, when Mom would pack our lunches, and every Wednesday it was puky Liverwurst sand-wiches, which meant every Wednesday it was just eat-the-Hostess-whatever and toss the sandwich, and then go home and tell Mom the liverwurst was delicious, but only if she asked.

{24}

I start edging away now, slowly, on my crappy bike, while my Mom continues to stand there, shielding her eyes from the fire ball sun.

"What exactly does I don't know mean, Randy?" Mom blurts out before I can get a head start worth anything.

"What?" I ask, circling back.

"Are you saying he didn't go to Wonderland Mall?" she asks, trying to trip me up, I just know.

"I didn't say he didn't go to Wonderland Mall, and I didn't say he did go. All I said was who knows."

My Mom bunches up her face then, which means she's close to being "at the end of my rope" which is what she says whenever she's about to burst and is fed up with everything. "Honestly Randy, if I wanted a runaround I would have asked for it!" she blurts.

"Well I'm going down to Norm's now, OK, because it's too darn hot talkin' in the sun and Norm has A/C" I say, finally pushing off and away. I don't bother looking back 'cause I can't say anymore without saying way too much.

I pound at Norm's screen door about a thousand times but nobody answers. Now I'm stuck. Every friend I have disappeared with Russell except Norm, who's missing, and maybe Taylor Parks, who doesn't really count, since he was really just a school friend, which means something's wrong with him enough that there's no way you'd want to even see him after school. With Taylor it was his stuttering and also that he could never remember anything said or taught to him, even if it happened a second ago.

So I'm stuck, with the sun shooting through me, and no way am I going home to get grilled some more by my Mom, just so I can sit and wait for my Dad to get home from golf, so he can grill me too.

I decide to go to Korvette's, which is just a half-a-mile, even less if you walk and hop the wall and go in the back way. Yeah, Korvette's will do 'cause it's close and air-conditioned, and kind of like Kmart, only better, because they always have all the latest albums with sales every week on them.

* * * * * *

I lock my bike up to the rack outside the doors at Korvette's. I feel the rush and vacuum sound of cold air hit me as I edge past a customer coming out. I take the escalator up to go look at the records, just to see what's new and what's old. What I really want is the new Beatles album, "Sgt Pepper's." If I really had some money I'd go back and buy all their albums before "Sgt. Pepper's" except the first one, "Meet The Beatles" because I have that one already.

But I don't have a red cent, as the saying goes. I just look at all the albums, kind of click off in my head ones I own, ones I have to buy next, and ones to ask for my birthday, which is comin' up soon.

Finally I decide it's no fun wanting, looking at records you have to wait for. Besides, wanting never got to owning, without money.

I go on over to sporting goods, thinking I'll just check out the baseball mitts. So I do. They have some really nice Rawlings mitts, especially the one signed by Brooks Robinson. My mitt is getting pretty worn out, but not in a good way, because worn out isn't worn in. Even linseed oil doesn't help anymore.

I head over to the bike section next and find myself standing in the aisle looking down at a whole row of shiny Schwinn's, from Stingray's all the way up to some ten-speeds. I look at all these Schwinn's and then think of my bike downstairs, out on the sidewalk, with its worn out paint, its dented fenders, and a big bubble of inner-tube bulging out the front tire, and it's like comparing diamonds to rocks.

{26}

I roll out a ruby red ten-speed from the line and try to situate myself on it, using a nearby display table to give me a boost.

"Can I help you, young man?"

I turn my head a bit and stare up at this giant salesman with a box head and one of those old fashioned hair cuts where if you wanted you could set a glass of water on it and never spill anything.

"I'm just lookin'," I say, which is what all kids say when they want out of the heat for a spell. I swear though, when I'm grown up and have lots of money bulging out of my wallet, I'm gonna come back here and when the salesman asks the same question I'm just gonna say: "When I'm good and ready!"

"Is your Dad or Mom around?" the giant asks, which doesn't surprise me any. That's always their next question. The third question isn't usually any question at all except to just tell you: "Hit the road, Jack!"

"My Mom is downstairs, looking at shorts" I lie, only because I know what's coming.

"Is that right?" he asks.

"Uh huh, and my Dad is over in records looking for some Sinatra album" I say, rolling my lie.

"Sinatra, I see" he says, and it doesn't look like he's gonna boot me out, and I'm not really big on lying, so I decide to be honest.

"You know, I really want a ten-speed but…"

But you can't reach the pedals yet, right? That's not a problem I can't fix. If you can hold on a sec you'll see" he says, looming over me.

"Well…"

"Just hold on a second and I promise you'll be surprised" he says, then disappears to the back, through the swinging doors where they keep everything. Maybe this guy is OK, I think. Maybe I'll stick around to see the surprise, or should I just take off right now?

I wait. I push the ten-speed back in line. I tug on some streamers that hang off some handlebars on a stupid girl's bike.

"Now keep an open mind, son" the salesman says, returning with some tools. He pulls a bike from the middle of the line, adjusts the handlebars down, then the seat. "Consider this ten-speed! This here is a 24 inch ten-speed. It's just as good as the bigger ones and still has all ten-speeds. Go on, hop on up, see if it fits!" he smiles.

So I do. And he's right. It fits perfectly. "Oh yeah, mister, this is great!" I yelp.

"See, and you can touch your feet to the ground and stand when you want, and now you can keep pace with everybody if you want, and I can see you're gettin' too old for that baby bike you probably got out front, right?"

"I like it a lot mister. I just have to talk my Dad into it and I'll be back in a flash!" I promise.

"You do that son! Just ask for me when you come back. Name's Phil."

I bolt down the escalator and come out to my scraggly bike, but I don't feel scraggly. I feel pretty good. Sometimes it seems that when you're looking for an answer you can't find it unless somebody finally says: "Hey Dummy, it's right in front of you!" And pretty much it was that giant salesman who showed me, even though all I had to do was look at all the bikes closer and there it was. A 24 inch ten-speed, yeah, it was that simple! Now I'd never fall behind. Now I could keep up with all my friends, even go neck-to-neck with Russell, no problem! And now there'd be no more "I don't knows" to my Mom 'cause Russell and me would make a pact. Now we {28} could ride as far and as long as we wanted, just go on-and-on, come back before the street lights blinked on, that's all!

I push off on my 20 inch bike, round the wall of Korvette's, and count the revolutions of the small sprocket, maybe for the last time. With my new bike I'll quit counting. I'll shift up, I'll shift down. And if I have to stop quick, I won't have to kick back on my coaster brake like some little kid. I'll just squeeze my hand brakes easy- like and come to a stop with class.

I wind around onto Sarasota now, then on to Salem, my street. I come to a stop at Norm's and glance on down the block to my house. I can see my Dad's car out front. Now what? If Russell isn't home yet it'll be both Mom and Dad grillin' me with "Where's Russell?"

I knock on Norm's door even though his house looks empty. C'mon Norm, open your door! C'mon Norm, for once in your life be home when I need you to be home! I think. But nobody answers. I really have to go home. Maybe they won't even bug me at all and

I can eat my dinner in peace and then work on Dad to get me my bike, tonight?

I stare once more down my block, hoping I'll spot Russell, but Russell isn't anywhere.

I pull into my driveway and rest my bike against the porch. I pull open the screen door hoping to see Russell explaining himself to Dad and Mom. Instead it's Dad not at his usual spot after golf, at the dining room table with a mug of beer, and my Mom, not in her summer spot, hovering over the ironing board, wearily. No, it's Mom and Dad together, holding onto each other, with Mom sobbing and Dad silent, a rock—something to hold tight to, forever, without Russell.

{29}

BROCK MARIE MOORE

Hemophilia

While passing a woman on the street, I feel
the sudden, ludicrous urge to bite her
to suck from her veins her dreams, successes,
her confidence
stealing her immunities to stanch my still-bleeding failures
devouring her strength
to rebuild the fallen city of my heart

Literary and Fine Art Magazine of Champlain College

BROCK MARIE MOORE

Fae

As we drive past the carnival
neon bursts in my brain
and my bones become the ferris wheel

my skeleton flares orange at the spine
hot pinkness creeps
  along the ulnae tubes
tiny mercury-misted phalanges explode green
into round glow-bulb fingertips

and my blood fizzes into lightness
particles excited impossibly bright

  then flicker flicker
  and we are past

CLARA BARNHART
4 AM

The sky is mauve.
The leaves are burgundy and plum, the distant
lights are marigolds,
with four star spiked petals glowing thick
like oil paint, with the shallow
luminescence of candle flames
burning in the dark. The silhouette
of a body in my bed-sheets, black
wrapped in fabric bunched and
cloaked Egyptian.
His eyes the shining black of beetle shells,
my hairline dampened by the labor of dreams
Hands skate
across my skin
loose across my hip, settle
on my rump   .
and I coo.
I am the mare with nostrils flared
he is a dog
and I am his chair.
My neck, the chew marked arm,
the soft white stuffing that he nuzzles with his muzzle.
We are
overlapping limbs and
dreary eyed kisses barely touching lips and
my ponytail curled around his chin,
like a husky sleeping in the snow.
We are each the other's yawn
in early morning.

CLARA BARNHART

Sunday School

I was baptized in a mountain spring
Alongside my cousin, Nick
My mother was the saint that spread
Holy water across my head, her fingernails
Filed and the half-moons white and freed
From her cuticles.
She always said she wasn't sure
About god.
The pads of her fingers are dry
From dish soap
Cheap soap,
Apple cider vinegar and water cleans
Windows and counter tops,
Whole milk is good for the bones.
Children
Are gifts from god she would say,
If god is up there.
Her touch feels like, what a cloud
Looks like, same as sticking your hand in a pot of
Flour and feeling it
Sift
Through the tucked and folded skin hidden in
Hard to reach places.
She would let me fall asleep with my hand
On her neck in the soft rounded special spot
Under her chin where
I could feel the steam of her pulse rising
Dancing along with our dreams, heartbeats

Aligned and in rhythm.
She and her sister that baptized their baby dolls
Here, at the spring,
The water sprouted form the earth and fed their family,
They cupped it in their palms and splashed their faces flushed,
And pink, two little girls in paisley dresses, saddle shoes,
Hair combed by the cornstalks they cut through,
Hands sticky with the sweat of holding another.
It was the clearest coldest water in the whole wide world.
It was infected
With E Coli
Some years later.
My brother helped my cousin Nick rebuild.
They fastened a cover,
To keep the bad things out, but
Sometimes I move the rocks that hold it down,
Stick my head in their, dip
The tips of my hair in the water until
The loose S's and J's in the strands will unravel
And fray like a rope
Unwound
At the end.
I listen to the echo
Of the water buried deep,
Churning,
Blurping,
Writhing in the stomach of the ground.
This is where god would come
If he was thirsty,
If he could be thirsty.

DAVID LAWRENCE

A Coffee Break

I go downstairs to Starbucks to get an iced coffee grandé
And two vanilla scones.
They offer three for the price of two
But I don't like discounts.
You get what you pay for in life
And then you die.
There used to be a sales girl there who was my friend.
She called me grandpa and gave me free coffee.
I accept gifts.
Free is not a cheap man trying to save a dollar.
Free is the air you breathe when the aftertaste
Doesn't remind you that you are separate from it.
I am back in my office trying to write something about
The experience of going to Starbucks
For no reason.
Everything fascinates me.
I can't stop talking about what I see coming and going
And that at sixty-two I am surely going.
I've enjoyed this life like a lemon.
I purse my lips
And suck in the tart misbehavior of my years.
I'd like to send a thank you note to myself for having been
So daring.
But I know I could have done better.
I could have crashed that car at seventeen into a tree and
Rode my dashboard to heaven.

{35}

DAVID WAITE
After A Party

Sunday morning they go out for breakfast
after waking, their skin still teased with beer,
changed into pajamas and thick, blue sweatshirts
they eat eggs against a sickness, slices of toast
soak between their white teeth,
half asleep until they're sipping
sugared coffee from a percolator,
bagels, pancakes and thin bacon
with drops of maple syrup.
they let it run into their stomachs,
they hold their heads to stop the throbbing and
the habit is lovely, talking over
the late night dance contests,
they're very polite
they tip too much,
they drop each other off
one by one and they're happy;
with still some work left for classes,
they walk to the shower and water starts
to soak their dry hair and bodies,
drops fall in their mouths and they're contented
humming new songs from the radio
with softer throats, deep, knowing
sleepy grins on their clean faces.

{36}

EMMA MARIE DEVINE

Dear Molly

speak out loud. yell
at the people around you; yell
at the open air.
tell everyone
how you feel hate
for your solid skin, hard boned limbs.
how you hurt
when you think of his body
tangled in the dashboard;
how you find yourself
crying
when you're alone.

tell them how you can feel
the hairs on the back of your neck rise
and how you crack your knuckles
when eyes that sink into wrinkled faces
sympathize.

be embarrassed
for those who can not
express the pain.
be unimpressed with those
who do not attend
the final farewell
and sit among the photos
of fifteen years at deer camp in dorset
at the church where you watch

{37}

a mother clutch and stain
her sons football jersey with tears.
be ecstatic
when you see the faces
of those who do.

do not shy away
from car rides
to smoke joints,
to go to burr and burton for class,
to go to dinner.

do not restrict
yourself
from thinking of his body
between the seat and the dashboard;
of his sister
still breathing
next to him.

restrict yourself
from not considering
your own young body
in that car;
from those adult eyes
on someone else's
breathing, hunting, woodworking
body.
and restrict yourself
from the windshield
with your seatbelt.

{38}

ERICA ROSI
Watching the Water

Someone threw a white stone into this pool.
Solid, it shines with thin sheets of mica.
Bird forms pass like clouds across the surface.
A running dog pounds currents of wakefulness
                              from surface to mud.

There are twenty-five adults
from many cultures and each one
                         resonates.
As I pass out the English worksheet, some grab eagerly,
some mumble thank-you, some hold up two palms
and I lay it across both, like food.

Someone threw a white stone into this pool.
In twos or threes, transparent minnows
                        leave wakes
of delicate, swaying time.
Their reflected scales trade tones with the mica.

When I re-enter the separate room
where the reading students are,
Asha cranes her neck,
                 pushes upward
her wrinkled face. She was late
and she wants me to recognize her presence.

Someone threw a white stone into this pool.
To take a stick and feel the heavy water's reality

always holds a slim edge of surprise.
A sense of longing arrives as the hand, with ease,
                         passes through the water.

Many gangly movements of arms and heads
when people pack their bags and put on jackets.
The jackets and bags hold them back,
                stall them, create
        backward rhythm
before the forward rush.
The class vanishes
with the last student's footstep through the door.

Someone threw a white stone into this pool.
Bird forms pass across the surface
and their shadows are

{40}

                    adrenalin.
A hand passes through and plays with the mud,
fingers lightly spaced like a sieve.

ERIN GLEESON
Coosane House

The rain knows this house well; it knows the patched white-stucco exterior, it knows the cerulean blue border above the doorway, the one that matches the short wooden fence surrounding the front, behind the shrubbery, which is home to a ram's skull decorated into the hedge—the shrubbery which is home to little al-ice-blue and cotton-white flowers. Yes, the rain knows this house. It has danced along its slate shingled-roof, one newer to the ancient weather's memory. It's pitter-pattered against the windows shielded by Irish lace, windows who are display cases to figurines: a ceramic Mother Mary, a staple in any county home. And the front walk; the rain has collected in the ruts, the dips and dents in a patch-worked pathway. It pools around the cornflower-blue ce-ramic tile, mosaiced within the grey-stone pieces. Other patches claim the color of rose, and my favorite few— harboring nautical sketches of boats and waves. The rain knows this path, this eclec-tic collection of colors and tiles, a speckled and cracked founda-tion beneath the feet of visitors and those who know it so well. The rain has known this house for hundreds of years. It knows the gates, the fields, and the stream that field-straw boats have sailed in. It knows the stinging nettle, and the dock-leaf growing beside it. It knows the mountains guarding from behind, and the latching green gate keeping vigil from the road; it knows Rover, the dog shepherding the sheep and hearts of old men. The rain knows the old tractor in the field; it's left its signs of moss and rust, which have made home along its metal jacket and old wheels, roving through its aged body. The rain has been here before; it's left its liquid song. I've been here before, too.

The drizzle may have found its way inside, during the days of thatched roofs or broken slate, but it is not as well acquainted with the interior as I. I'm not sure it has fallen against the stained-glass squares of the window in the white front door, which hides beneath its own shelter of stone and stucco. Nor has it painted itself over those worn goldenrod walls. I'm quite sure it has not taken hold of the warm knob, letting itself in.

The rain wants to know what dwells inside, because it leaves one curious to know only part of a whole so well. It begins to wonder about the other half, and so it clings to my clothes, my raincoat, my sea-blue scarf; it settles itself into the copper rings of my hair and holds tight to my eyelashes. I track puddles behind me, on the honey-brown linoleum floor. To my left, a small room, never used, and a flight of steep and narrow stairs, leading way to bedrooms in which teams of children have lived, where my grandfather lived, where my father lived, where his beloved grand- {**42**} father dwelled, too. Straight ahead leads to the kitchen, tiled in grey-blue, burnt orange and cream. A kitchen too small to actu- ally use, too crowded and cluttered to try to use. There are bags of potatoes, an old oven, a portable stove-top, mops and brooms older than I, white tiled walls against green, and a goldenrod ceiling. It is a kitchen that has not been used for a kitchen's purpose since matriarchy reigned. And a bathroom off to the side, with the yellowing mirror and petite porcelain toilet bowl; there is a white stream of grey-day light shining through the tiny window.

Alas, the rain does not take any one of these routes. It fol- lows the tingling warm scent, a true comfort-scent, of a freshly lit peat-fire. We veer to the right, into the still-pumping heart of the house. Not much bigger than the rest of the rooms, this one is a living memory—the kind one cannot shake from their minds like rain from a coat. I remove my jacket, brushing rain from my hair, and sit in a throne of shabby-scarlet and chipped wood.

This room is years of mothers, fathers, children and welcomed strangers. The fading floor has worn the tracks of dirt and grass and manure. The cushions on each chair are certainly lived-in. On the wall is a mirror and above that mirror on the wall is wedged a fading palm-leaf folded into the shape of a cross. Along the walls are clocks, calendars, an old lamp and a framed painting of Jesus, illuminated by a plastic red light bulb. There is a radio, older than myself, sitting on a metal chair. African relics are scattered around the room; they are figurines that have traveled with a priest brother. A large cerulean hutch sits in the corner, shelving boxes of Barry's tea, cups and glasses, jars of spices and spreads, tins of biscuits, cookies and breads, and bottles and bottles of spirits; whiskey, scotch and some "real old mountain-dew"–Irish moonshine. Beside the hutch, next to the one window, is a folding table for sitting, eating and talking of Christian flaws, dwindling economies and mingled memories.

Demanding the attention of the room is the fireplace. How does one paint a picture of such a fireplace? It has the face of the old men who stoke it. It is covered in a medley of moss-green, grey, cream and copper and brown, with patches of robin-egg blue. Arms hang from the hearth: one with hooks for pots, which get more use than anything in the kitchen, one from a poker and other tools, and one from which a bulky set of binoculars hang. On the floor sits the teakettle and pots. Against the wall stands a hand-carved blackthorn hiking cane with bumps and knobs, though it's smooth to the touch. And there, on the wooden boards, is "cat," who finds warmth and solace next to the growing fire. This one-eyed, aged, golden feline breaks the guard of old countrymen, these old bach-elors, receiving scraps and affectionate clicks and clucks.

These countrymen are the voices and creaks in this house: My kindred-spirit teacher, the silent millionaire, the laughing deaf husband, and the timid host–brothers of my gentle spoken and mischievous-eyed grandfather. They are bits and pieces of my father. They are bits and pieces of me. They are the old house, as I must be. I remain in my scarlet throne and listen to the rain, outside, dancing on the slate roof and on the shadow-box windows, falling into puddles on nautical tiles. Falling towards patchwork fields and mountains and streams. Falling, outside, against trees and wooden ladders, fences and shrubs, rams and sheep and their bleating young. Falling on a house—Coosane—beyond three hundred years, tucked between a mountain and a latching, swinging green gate

{44}

FRED YANNANTUONO

Agita Villagio

The fazool tastes like filings,
The pasta like cork,
The pizza's repulsive,
The waiter's a dork.

The barkeep's a wiseass,
The waitress a pill.
The chef is a guy
I would sure like to kill.

The owner's a doofus.
To come here I dread.
They can't even bake
An acceptable bread.

I'd go round the corner
To McAlloon's Pub.
The problem's they dish out
An even worse grub.

FREDERICK ZYDEK

Playing the Bass Viola

This is music one must stand or sit behind.
Its messages come deep from the center
of the earth - tones so low they can carry

the music of the spheres upon their backs.
Pluck the strings and a bass viol sounds like
timpani enriched with the entire chromatic scale.

Use the bow and it yawns deep from the gut.
This is music that knows the secrets of lost
things and what it feels like to find a light

{46}

in the window but no one home. You would
expect this music to grunt and groan coming
from giants in the back row as it does, but

more often than not, it is played just under
the melody, behind the scenes or to the side
of the main event the way a distant thunder

lets you know it's there without calling too
much attention to itself. This music casts
beautiful shadows and reminds every tune

it attends that no matter how fresh the music,
there will always be a few ghosts wandering
through it looking for things to call their own.

FREDERICK ZYDEK

Sipping a Sauvignon Blanc Over Pork Chops

There's a butteriness to this wine, hints of basil,
coriander, tarragon and thyme, a touch of green
olive, a smoky flavor that gives a simple chop
the elegance of Vietnamese and Thai cuisine.

France may have been its home but once it began
exploring the world, dishes once native to Japan,
Korea, Mexico and China quickly learned to say
its name. I've known some that even went well

with pan-fried eggplant and sausages made of veal.
But it is the pork chop that turns it from a living
room to a dining room wine at my house. I have
friends who will not drink it, ostentatious folk who

claim the Fume Blanc is vastly superior. They have
no idea that in the 1960s someone simply began
marketing Sauvignon Blanc under a new name. I
seldom correct them and never invite them to dinner

when we're having pork chops. What I like best
about these wines is that new lovers of the fruit
of the vine can always find one that suits their palate,
one whose grassy mysteries invite them back to taste

and taste again. It always comes with surprises,
a faint essence of pepper-melons, an elegance that
reminds one of a chateau in France, aromatic bits
of freshly-turned soil and crisp green apples.

{47}

GARY SILVA
Engine Trouble

The oil pressure drops as you cross the orange bridge
spires floating among the clouds,
and as you slow among fifty zipping Buicks and Hondas,
the pit of your thrilled stomach turns metallic.

But the electric windows are still working
so you roll them up, upside down guillotines
cutting the crap,
                              and the clouds
lower themselves to cover all of the span
while your eyelids fall, too, heavy as Vaseline.

Two teenagers walk on the pedestrian strip
throwing crumbs to the seagulls
with the gallon of gas in hand they siphoned out
of your tank.

You don't care, so you sit in your gray velour
driver's seat and stare down the three laned road
at the approaching tow truck, yellow, its scorpion
stinger dangling stupidly.

{48}

JAN JOHNSON

Lucky

I don't even know what time I laid down last night. After
those Tele-thon guys. And Chitty Chitty Bang Bang on cable. And
Saturday Night Live. I am trying to cut down on my TV but it is
my only comfort since the trouble began at Bingo Night.

He didn't even register on my radar but Shirlene saw him immedi-
ately and nearly had a fit. "He's so cute!" She nudged me to look
to our left.

I am not sure I would call him particularly cute. He was a
little guy, more suited to Shirlene's size than mine. But he had
a square jaw and still had his hair. His teeth were a little yel-
low and he wore baggy shorts with a Hawaiian shirt. And Birken-
stocks with socks.

{49}

"G-2," the caller said and Shirlene didn't even check her card.
"Is it hot in here or what?" Shirlene fanned herself with her
card, letting all the markers fall off.

Shirlene has been my best friend ever since the fourth grade
when she moved in next door here in Peers and changed my lonely
life. Shirlene is the one who calls me up and says "get off
your ass! Let's go out and have some fun!" She is the one who
discovered Bingo Night on Tuesdays at the Canadian Legion in Eldon
and convinced her uncle who served in the Faulklands to get us a
pass inside.

In a town like this there's only so much action and Shirlene
says you got to go throw yourself into the center of it if you
hope to meet any decent men. If you go to the bars, you get about
20 roughnecks from the drilling crews asking you to dance and you
know what else. Also, she says you've got to do things you enjoy
and meet men who enjoy the same pastimes or your relationship will
 -homa. And their talk is big and loud and full of wise cracks

be doomed. She reads a lot of those magazines that tell you these things. I myself depend on cable TV and when I dream, I do not dream of men in Hawaiian shirts at the Canadian Legion Hall in Eldon; I dream about Hawaii itself.

When somebody yelled "bingo," we all moaned and spilled the markers off our cards. It was Shirlene's turn to go up to the bar to buy us another round of Caesar's and a bag of ketchup chips. So I was alone. I had just had a dream of Hawaii last night. In it, Shirlene and I waited for one of those big canoes to ferry us to our hotel and I was afraid to go off into the ocean in that big-to-me-but-small-to-the-sea vessel. When we got there safe, we had to carry our luggage on this thin little walkway to the hotel and by the time I finally got to my room, there were people in it -- an old couple, napping on both the beds. When I first turned on the light, I thought they were dead. Then I woke up.   {50}

Still, the dream of Hawaii is strong, even the scary and icky parts so I bought $10 worth of lottery tickets on the hope of striking it rich and sat down at a table scratching them off until I tossed my last, losing lottery ticket into the pail on the table and said "Shirlene, a fat lot of luck I'm having to-night" but the person who pulled out the chair and sat down next to me wasn't Shirlene.
It was him.

******

"Why what a pleasant surprise!" Shirline fluttered about arranging chairs like a bird making a nest when she saw who was at the table.

Shirlene offered him her Caesar but he said he didn't drink. "I'm a teetotaler," he said in his American accent. But not the accent of the roughnecks – most of them come from Texas or Okla-homa. And their talk is big and loud and full of wise cracks about Canadians while his talk was so quiet we had to lean forward just to hear him. Around here, the roughnecks book up all the motels, eat breakfast every morning at Clyde's, then come back from drilling around suppertime to drink. Oil hits $60 a barrel and Shirlene and I know we're out of the bars unless we want trouble, that's for sure.

His name was Brian and he was traveling through Canada on bike.

"Bicycle! Why that's a lot of work!" Since Brian sat down with us, everything Shirlene said seemed punctuated by an exclamation mark.

"But it's slow. I get to meet people. Look around. Sometimes I go only five miles a day."

He said he planned to spend a year on the trip. He said back home in the Bay Area, he played folk music on guitar at festivals and farmers' markets. He also gave lectures on native plants of the Anza Borrego in Southern California.

Shirlene's couldn't take her eyes off him. "You can make a living doing that?"

He shook his head. "I have investments."

I looked at him. He was tan and his legs and shoulders were muscled from months of bicycling and he had a good laugh, a real laugh that sounded like he agreed what was said was funny. I looked around the legion hall at guys with big guts and too much aftershave and their shirts buttoned open at least one button beyond what they should have and knew exactly what she saw him in. But still I looked at him from the side of my eye. "How'd you get in here? You got an uncle in the Canadian Legion?"

******

Shirlene ran to the other end of the shuffleboard table where we were trying to play and said "Darla, Brian has an interest in all the Tim Horton's in Alberta!"

"How do you know?"

"He told me!"

I looked at him. The tan and the muscles also came with a beard. Longish hair. Dirty clothes. Rank smell. "He looks like he's homeless."

Shirlene looked at him over her shoulder. He raised his orange juice to her. She turned her face to me. "Think of it! If I marry him, you can have all the free soup you want. Coffee too. And doughnuts! Darla, you can have all the free doughnuts you want!"

I suspected that it would not be free doughnuts but instead a lot of nights home alone watching cable while Shirlene ignored me to pursue a man. I flicked my wrist and kicked her butt at another round of shuffleboard.

{52}

"Darla, you have been practicing."

"Just lucky is all."

"My turn." Brian replaced Shirlene at the end of the shuffle-board table and Shirlene sat down. We had to take turns playing one-against-one because we could not induce anyone else in the Canadian Legion Hall to make the game a foursome. Brian played especially badly. So bad that he seemed to be letting me win, which I took as an insult. He didn't let Shirlene win when they played.

Shirlene watched Brian and I face off against each other the length of a shuffleboard table apart. He definitely was letting me win. He had a weathered face but not an unpleasant one. A wide smile. He smiled often. Shirlene emptied her Caesar in a few quick swallows and waved down a busy waitress for another. "An-other round for all three of us," she said. "We're celebrating. My friend is lucky in love."

******

Two days later Shirlene and I met for lunch at Clyde's. I was
late. When I finally got there, Shirlene was halfway through a ham
sandwich in one of the booths by the glass that separates the res-
taurant part of Clyde's from the other part, a curling rink with
a long alley of ice in the wintertime but now just an empty and
forlorn alley with a case of mayo stored there for the restaurant.
She put down her sandwich. "Did he call you?"

"Sorry I'm late."

She sat forward and smiled, flashing her horsey teeth. "Did
he call you?"

I pulled out a menu, which was foolishness because we both
know everything Clyde's has to offer. Anyway, we always order the
same thing.

"Have you two gotten together?"

I looked away from her. I stared through the glass down
the long alley where Shirlene and I spent so many happy Sunday
nights on the ice in our curling league. Normally, I would have
called Shirlene immediately after he called. Once, I called her
at 1 a.m. knowing that she had to be in the office by 7 a.m. to
tell her about a night of particularly spectacular sex. Good
as the sex was, I couldn't wait for him to leave so I could call
Shirlene to tell her about it. But in the three days since we
met Brian, I hadn't called Shirlene. That's a long time for us.
I don't think we've gone that long without calling since my mom
denied me phone privileges for a week after Shirlene and I busted
up my mom's car our senior year in high school.

The day we ate lunch at Clyde's was the day Shirlene and
I were supposed to make our down payment on the Hawaii trip to
qualify for the reduced airfare. We were supposed to decide at
lunch whether we could afford to splurge on the deluxe accommoda-
tions with an ocean view or settle for the hotel two blocks from
the beach. We didn't even talk about Hawaii. She finished her ham

before my egg salad came and said she had to get back to work.

******

That first night with him in my apartment after the shuffle-
board at the legion hall, I woke with a start. Brian was watching
me. His brown eyes stared down in the moonlight. He said he had
been dreaming that it was my birthday and he didn't know it but
others did and came with presents. He wished he knew my birthday.

I started to tell him the date but he said he wished it were
written in ink on his calendar. In the dream, a man named Leo
commanded him to buy gargoyles, those stone guards from all dan-
ger. He wished my apartment was encircled by gargoyles. He said
he made a mental note that in the morning, he would buy gargoyles.

******

When the Hawaii trip with Shirlene fell through, I used the
money I had saved for it to fly down to Berkley every other week-
end. Brian flew up to Calgary the other weekends and I drove down
to meet him. He said meeting me cut off his bike tour of Canada
before the snow could. I said it was the Canadian Rockies.

"No. We had this chemistry. Romance should be in the here
and now. Just at this moment."

He spoke from his kitchen, where I sat on the cushioned bench
in one of his romantic bay windows. Outside the window, he grew
roses and the smell of roses wafted through the open window. At
that moment, I too wanted to be in the here and now.

"Here's your toothbrush. It's red. Mine's blue. I'll put it
right here," he said as he laid it on the shelf in the medicine
cabinet the first night I stayed over. We had just brushed our
teeth together in the nude, a more intimate act than the sex that

preceded it, a friendly act, a simple domestic everyday act that
we performed like children getting ready for bed, and I felt as
close to him as it is possible to feel about someone you just met
a couple weeks earlier.

All weekend we stayed in and cooked, or mostly he cooked in
his stainless-steel-and-black-appliances kitchen conjuring up
meals from scratch that tasted of ginger, garlic and rosemary.
When we ran out of saffron on a dreary, cold Sunday morning we
walked side-by-side and close enough to both enjoy the shelter
of the small umbrella and each other's body heat, laughing almost
the whole way to his newest, favorite shop. At the shop, I was
stunned at all you could buy to cook with in Berkley – not just
fresh saffron but also ginger root and different types of olive
oil. Except you couldn't buy ketchup chips to save your soul.

"Must be a Canadian delicacy," he said.

"I s'pose."

{55}

The next weekend he flew north but we didn't stay in Calgary.
Instead we drove over to Banff and stayed in a lodge in the park.
Those mountains just fill the windshield of my Datson and I can
never get enough of them. Shirlene and I have camped beside moun-
tain lakes and watched the full moon rise over the fir trees and
reflect with all the contours – those patches of gray within the
white – back on the water. We have sat over sweet-smelling fires
in perfect silence. We have swum in cold mountain lakes.

Brian and I ate pan-fried trout in the dining room while
watching elk come right up to the huge windows of the lodge. Fall
comes early up here and the males had begun the rutting.

I watched those elk and thought to myself that maybe sex is
in the here and now but a relationship requires a future? It was
the kind of thing I would have said to Shirlene and she would have
let loose with a whole philosophy to back up what I just thought

in passing. I wished she were here in the lodge at Banff right now. Shirlene and I had come to Banff to camp every September when the tourists started to thin out but this year I came with Brian.

On Saturday, while Brian and I hiked a trail around the lake I could have sworn I saw Shirlene. Again that same afternoon, in the parking lot, I thought I recognized a headful of frizzy brown curls emerge from a familiar Toyota. Then, on Sunday just after we checked out, in the gift shop at the lodge, I knew the figure at the cash register. "Shirlene! What are you doing here?"

"What do you mean 'what am I doing here?' I come here every september."

But usually she came with me. Shirlene anticipated my question.

"Julie Taylor and I are staying at the South Shore campsite. Where are you camping?"

"Actually, we're staying in the lodge." I hated to tell Shirlene I was staying here in this swank joint while she and Julie slept on the ground. I expected her to say something like: "Well la de da." But she didn't.

{56}

"See these earrings I bought? Aren't they cute?" Shirlene fished them out of her purse and dangled them before me. They were cute and I wanted a pair just like them so she showed me where to find them on the rack in the shop. We both thought purple looked best with my eyes.

"Or maybe the green? They're pretty too. You know, Darla, I'm in a conundrum. I feel like I have to tell you something. It's eating me alive. But I don't want to."

"What?" I looked at her in the reflection in the gift shop mirror.

"I don't know how to tell you this." Her face scrunched up.
"Just tell. You're in a conundrum."

She put the earrings down. "He has a girlfriend."

In the mirror, I watched suspicion form, not against Brian, but against Shirlene's motivations for telling me this. Was Shirlene just being frank? Or malicious? Was she jealous? Or was she protecting me? A wrinkle formed across my forehead which had no other wrinkles. My face in the mirror stared back childishly smooth, babyish. That lone crease of suspicion cut into the baby fat, a demarcation line, a line of no return. "Brian? A girl-friend? How would you know that?"

"Jeff and Jeanie Berkson. He stayed on their land when he was coming through on bike. He used their phone to call her. He called her everyday. She would call Jeff and Jeanie and leave messages for him. She still talks to Jeanie and Jeanie likes her. Her name is Barbara."

The line across my forehead deepened with the pronunciation of her name. "How could he have a girlfriend if I'm at his house every other weekend?"

Shirleen's face in the mirror had wrinkles. We were the same age but she had more experience, more to show of her life on her face. "It's a different country. They do things different down there. They're not Canadians."

The following Friday when I returned to Berkley, the red toothbrush was gone. There was only his single blue toothbrush in the medicine cabinet. I was mad at him for making the mistake of drawing my attention to it, then removing it. Or maybe it wasn't a mistake. Maybe it was a message?

I crawled into his great soft bed with the flannel sheets, the bed that I had slept so soundly in just two weekends earlier, thinking that I would ask him about the toothbrush when we were curled together that night.

But I didn't need to. He took me in his arms right away and told me about his friend. "Barbara. She's great. We're just friends. But, you know, she's great. She's a writer. A poet. And her poetry is great. She's also a homeless counselor. And

she's doing great at that." He paused. "I don't want to talk
about her anymore."

******

"All hardware must be removed when you enter this bed." He
dangled above me my earring, the one I bought with Shirlene at the
lodge gift shop in Banff.
"Did I poke you?" It was dark. I was sleepy and fuzzy in
thought.
"I heard it drop to the floor."
 I took out the other earring and laid both on the nightstand
beside the bed. Then we went back to sleep.
But that Sunday before I flew home, I left the earrings behind
on the nightstand as a test. I would ask him if he found them **{58}**
and if he said no and they were gone when I returned in two weeks,
I would know he had thrown them away. I would know he was hiding
me from Barbara. All week long I wished I had left a different
pair of earrings; I hated to lose those particular ones.

******

Being gone every weekend, I didn't see Shirlene. Even in a
small town, if you don't show up for Sunday night curling league
or make sure you're both taking lunch at the same time, you can go
a few weeks until you bump into each other. We finally did though,
in the dairy products section of the store where there was no saf-
fron or fresh ginger. We were both out of milk.
"How's Brian?"
"He's okay." The day before he had brought me breakfast in
bed. Scrambled eggs, seasoned to perfection. Fried potatoes,
also seasoned to perfection. Fresh orange juice. Good coffee

made in a press. He cleaned up the kitchen from the night before
while I ate alone in bed. "He cooks. He's a good cook"
  "You two getting serious?"
  "Oh it's just fun." Except it wasn't much fun.
  Really it wasn't as much fun as buying earrings in Banff with
a good girlfriend you could talk to. There are relationships that
are more intimate than sexual relationships. Yet I couldn't tell
her that. Instead, I talked as if I lived to commute between
Berkley and Calgary.
  "I s'pose. But you never get to spend a weekend home. You
have to travel every weekend while he gets every other in Berkley.
Doesn't he ever think of you?"
  "I don't mind. It's good to get out of town."
  "You could do curling league if you were around every other
Sunday night?"
  I didn't know how to tell her that I couldn't afford curling
league now that all my disposable income went to Alaska Airlines.

  But Shirlene was right; I did want a weekend at home after so
many away. I did want to sleep in on Saturday and hang around in
sweats with no makeup puttering in the apartment. I wanted to
have a day in which I didn't have to scrape ice off the windshield
of the car. I wanted a day with no car in it.
  After work on Friday, I dreaded having to take a bath and
drive all the way to Calgary to get in at 9:30 p.m. to meet him
at the airport. A light snow was falling but it looked like the
kind that could turn into a pretty good storm with time. As the
windshield wipers sqwooshed, I wondered what became of the ear-
rings? He hadn't mentioned them on the phone. I didn't ask, but
I expected him to say "I found your earrings."
  It would have satisfied me for some time if he had said "they
make me think of you" or "you look so beautiful in them" or some

endearment that brought the earrings back to me, to his interest
in me.

The snow fell harder and I turned on the radio to get a
weather report. But the deejay prattled on about weekend enter-
tainment in Calgary. Lots of live music and even a meeting of a
native plant society. I laughed out loud. Weekend entertain-
ment. With another woman for the week. Barbara. Or is she
another woman? Is she one of several? I mean, he's looking. He
must be looking. He called me.

Halfway to Banff my cell phone rang. Service isn't much good
up north, but it starts coming in down around Edmonton. It was
Brian saying he wasn't coming after all. "Russ asked me to go
camping. It's been years since we've done that."

"It's November. Won't it be too cold?"

"We're going south. The Anza Borrego. He wants to be in
nature. He wants to travel. He wants to live in the moment."

{60}

"Don't we all."

"You okay? You sound funny."

"Did you find my earrings?"

"Yes. They were on the nightstand. I mailed them to you."

******

So I'm watching TV. I've wracked up a good-sized credit card
debt to Alaska Airlines with all this flying around. He hasn't
called and I haven't called him.

Shirlene understands completely that I'm too broke for Bingo
Night anymore. Now we watch cable at my apartment on Tuesday
nights and eat ketchup chips and make our own Caesar's unless
she pays for my Bingo. She loaned me money for curling league on
Sundays.

"Well it was mistake. I have no luck in love." I fingered the earrings.

Shirlene shook her head. "You were lucky! You got out before you ended up with him. A cute man with an inherited fortune's no keeper. He'll cheat on you and break your heart because he has nothing better to do."

I looked out the window at the snow piling up in the parking lot. "Same can be said for working men. So you think it's just us girls?"

"Nah. Romance is no better than friendship and friendship's no better than sex -- although if you ask me, any relationship that's got a future trumps all."

{61}

JASON WILKINSON
Take Life By The Nut-Sack

And run with it until the putrefied bits slip
through your fingers
causing infections to spread
like gossip over them
staining your clothes

Run with it until it dries in your hands
though it were no more than powder
and the hair upon that scrotum
has desiccated beyond recognition

Until you no more notice the stench of it
than that of a dead fly
entombed beneath the azaleas
and pedestrians are obliged to wear protective gear
lest you should contaminate them unawares

Run with the precious nickel bag
twisting every last demand from its host
-bury your nails in supple flesh
if only to exact more and more

Take Life by the nut-sack and wear it on a chain
next to the promise rings and that fake shark tooth
your uncle Dougie swore came from 'a big one'
he caught off the coast of Jamaica last spring

Take Life by the nut-sack and treat it like a prostitute
dragging it through the streets
at the ends of frayed tethers

Use its head for a battering ram
against hard-to-open doors

Take Life by the nut-sack without compunction
or delusion
or the occasional hangover

Take Life by the nuts
and unto those testes
do what Conscience dictates
must be inflicted upon no other.

{63}

JAY BLAISDELL
The Secret Annex

In basic training at Fort Benning, I told myself I was a boy, so that I could do more push-ups, sprint faster, and not be intimidated by these country fucks from east Kentucky who never crapped into porcelain growing up. I deepened my voice, hawked and spit, and cinched my eyebrows on the firing range. No one but the drill sergeant spoke to me. In advanced individual training, I started acting like a girl again, and these east Kentucky hayseeds would beg to kiss me and wouldn't stop. Finally, I let this guy name Dillon stick his tongue in my mouth, and he pulled his willy out and asked me to kiss it.

"Kiss an inch, blow a mile," I said.

"Izzat a yes?"

"No!" I smacked him. "Go back to your livestock."

Of course, it's different when you're in love. The last time Dillon called, I was at my first station, the 254th Base Support Battalion in the Netherlands. He said he'd been deployed to Af- ghanistan. "We're all locked behind this fence—one big cage in the desert." I kissed the phone and told him I missed him, and he gave me his "Ava Sweet-sweet" in an accent thick as Kentucky sorghum. "It's only six months."

I asked him for his e-mail address, and he said he didn't have computer access yet. I started sniffling.

"Ava, shhhhhhh." He sighed. "Sweetie, you can write me a let- ter the old-fashioned way." He gave me his mailing address, and I tucked it somewhere safe—so safe that even I couldn't find it after I'd written him a five-page letter and tried to mail it.

It's true. I have a talent for losing important things: debit cards, night vision goggles, marriage licenses, plane tickets, husbands. But I also have trenchant insight into matters of the

heart and spirit. I know, for instance, that a woman can be a
devout Catholic and a Jew simultaneously. Like most Catholic Jews,
I lose things because I'm preoccupied with homogenizing opposites
into a unified whole. For instance, Catholic Jews believe that
Jesus saved humanity from approximately half its sins. The other
half are chronic in nature—confessable and treatable, but far from
forgivable. My patron Saint, Anne Frank, is the probably the most
famous Catholic Jew. Most people seem to forget that she celebrat-
ed Christmas in 1944.

Though I can't prove it, I was married in Denmark. I don't
remember exactly where, because Dillon was driving and I was try-
ing to decide if I should take his last name. I had known other
female soldiers who had tied the knot, and everyone still called
them by their maiden name.

And since I didn't take Dillon's last name and had no pic-
tures of him—just memories and a crock-pot he gave me to soften
beans—my colleagues had a tough time believing that I was, in
fact, married, that I had misplaced my husband as easily as a
mailing address. They began rumors that I was in league with an
imaginary friend, that I was "disturbed." I suppose I was. I
searched for Dillon for almost a year, making calls to his family,
the military, the police. The last anyone knew, he had been medi-
cally discharged and was on his way back to east Kentucky.

I met my second husband on a Saturday morning train trip to
Amsterdam. My squad leader bought some group-rate tickets and
let anybody, civilian or military, sign up on the bulletin board
at the MP station. Generally, the weather in the Netherlands was
like the fine mist of a car wash, between cycles. But that day the
sun surprised us, bestowing its auspicious light on the glitter-
ing shoals of bicycles we passed in Eindhoven, on the canals near
Utrecht, and on the golden-haired legs of one Tyler Kossuth, sit-

ting in front of me. As I watched the interplay of green fields and calm water speeding past, he watched me cross my legs and bounce my foot. I had to go to the restroom. "Hi," he said, unabashedly gazing at my face. "Hi," I said, stepping over his shins and sandals.

Later, when I returned, he asked me about the birthmark on my calf. He said it looked "like a gazelle running" and demonstrated by squeezing the meat of my calf repeatedly. Our friends assumed that we knew each other.

Reaching Amsterdam, our group divided into smaller groups. We agreed to meet back at the train station and go to dinner somewhere. While the others wandered off to the red light district and the sex museums, Tyler and I headed for 263 Prinsengracht, the address where Anne Frank spent the last years of her life hiding from the Gestapo. We bought our tickets, and since the tour wouldn't begin for another hour, we sat on the edge of a canal, next to a houseboat, eating frikadels heaped with onions.

{66}

"So why are you so bent on seeing Anne Frank?" he asked, lifting a miniature plastic fork to his mouth just as the meat fell onto his lap.

"My mother's Jewish," I said, though there was much more to it than that.

Muttering, he wiped mayonnaise from his shorts with a napkin. "That makes you Jewish?"

The houseboat started its engine, making the water boil and churn at my feet. "No," I said. "I don't know."

To get to "the Secret Annex," as our guide called it, we entered through a door that appeared to be a set of dilapidated bookshelves. The stairs, like those in my own Dutch rental, were very steep.

"You father isn't Jewish?" Tyler asked.

"Catholic," I said.

"My parents are Catholic." He glanced over the beds and walls without really seeing them.

"Still married?" I asked.

"Divorced," he said, peering into the water closet. "My dad was gone for almost two years during the Gulf War. I guess his career was more important. He's been a full-bird colonel for, what, six years now? He's sitting behind a desk at a NATO base. He'll never make general."

"My father was in the Gulf War, too," I said. "They kept extending his tour. My mother and I flew to Bahrain and drove to the U.S. consulate to demand that he come home."

Tyler laughed. "I'm sure that did a lot of good."

"They released him."

"Really," he said, eyebrow cocked. "Where's home?"

"England. Sicily, Japan, Canada."

We climbed the stairs to the third floor. He stood behind me, his chest touching my back. "Do you think Anne Frank felt at home here?"

This was the very room where the Franks and the Van Daans lived the last years of their lives, where Anne peeled potatoes, wrote poetry, and practiced French, where she argued with her mother and heard the BBC announce the liberation of North Africa, the surrender of Italy. This was where she began to bleed as a woman, where she fell in love with the only boy available. No, this was not her home. It was her universe. "Anne Frank's home was her diary," I said.

In the beginning, I was receptive to Tyler's discourses on the cultural opportunities of Europe. We saw symphonies in Aachen, operas in Paris. Most of the soldiers in my squad viewed our relationship as healthy. They said we were a good couple.

We ended up taking dancing lessons on Sunday nights.

It was a family-owned studio of three generations. Rene, the middle-aged Dutchman who taught the lessons with his wife, had black hair, a microphone on his shirt, and the beginnings of portliness. Tyler and I seldom understood him, but it didn't matter. We learned by imitation and came to prefer Rene's speaking in Dutch. His foreign syllables became a liturgy of sorts, allowing us a privacy that the other couples didn't have. For me, Sunday night was an intricate ceremony of transformation, a holy communion, a transfiguring of our carnal bodies into something higher, spiritual. Most lessons, we arrived early and parked next to a renovated Cathedral near the Maastricht Centrum. Once inside, we strolled down a long a corridor of photographs of dancers and sat at one of the round tables surrounding the dance floor. There we drank Chardonnay while a class of teenagers finished their lesson. They always seemed more adept than Tyler and I, turning in intricate patterns in the same unexpected directions. I felt envious at being older yet less experienced.

{68}

When the teenagers left and Rene started his liturgy on the microphone, Tyler pulled me onto the dance floor and put his hands on my body. And for that time only, we were a couple. The motion of his body warmed my insides like liquor. It was foreplay—foxtrot, tango, English waltz.

Ultimately, he damaged me. And when the lesson was over and he had left my bed, I smelled him on my hands and wept. From others, I learned that Tyler went to bed with a different girl almost every Friday night. Then he went to mass with his sister almost every Sunday morning. Far from being racked with guilt, he seemed too stupid for genuine contrition. "I'm young," he said, driving us from Brunssum to Maastricht for our lesson. "This is my moment."

"What—to be a hypocrite?" I covered my knees with my dress. "I'm young, too, and you don't see me sleeping with every guy who comes on to me."

"That's because you're married." He pushed down the sun visor.

"I just said that so these army fuck-heads would leave me alone."

"You're not married?"

"No."

"I knew it." He honked his horn and blinked his lights at the car in front of us.

"Tyler, your faith clearly says you should feel guilty."

"I can't help if I don't feel guilty." He swung into the left lane and passed the car in front of us.

"Then you don't believe what you profess to believe," I said.

"I don't profess anything." He slowed and downshifted.

"Why do you go to mass, then?"

"I'm Catholic. It's what Catholics do." He stopped at a red light. Several boys on bicycles passed in front of us.

"A Catholic playboy?"

"Ava, if you can be a Catholic Jew, then I can be me." The light turned green. He chirped the tires and rode the bumper of a car into the village of Nuth. We were already doing 70K.

"Tyler." I rubbed his leg.

He swerved. "Stop it."

"Have you been drinking?"

"What are you talking about?" He shifted gears. "Where in the Bible does it say you can't have sex before marriage?"

"I'm a Catholic Jew. We use the Newest New Testament."

"There's no 'we,' Ava! You're the only fucking Catholic Jew in the world! I'm not going to dance with you unless you stop this shit."

"Don't threaten me." I smacked his face.

"Do it again!" His nostrils flared. "See what happens."

"This isn't fun, Tyler. You keep threatening me."

"I'm not your boyfriend!"

"Why would I think that? You can't even commit to seventeen dance lessons!"

"Not with you." He drove the full circle of a roundabout, taking us back to Brunssum.

"I knew you'd do this. I'm just a piece of ass to you."

"It's dancing, Ava. Not marriage."

"You're unclean, Tyler. You're dancing with me and you're unclean."

He stepped out of the Volkswagen and slammed the door. I sat in the quiet cockpit as he strode across the wet lawn into his house. I lived down the street. After the dance lesson, he usually walked me home and slept with me, but not tonight. He expected me to follow him inside and repent. I climbed out of the car and thought of how different he seemed from that day in the Secret Annex. I remembered my own diary and the volumes of entries I had written to my future husband, whoever he might be. Was I so different now, so disillusioned and betrayed by circumstance, that I had given up completely? With the leaves whirling in little cyclones on the brick-paved parking spaces, and the street lights blinking on in succession, I decided that love, contrary to popular wisdom, was not about compromise. It was about insistence, persistence, "keeping the faith"—believing, despite the evidence, that the woman I was, imperfect though she may be, was worthy of a man who loved her. And as I watched for cars and crossed the street—as I fell in love with my new, old self—I saw an old, respectable lady waiting at the bus stop, a woman whom I did not know from Eve. I wished that she was about to discover true love. Yes, she was on her way.

In December, Tyler and I parted with a handshake. I didn't ask him for his e-mail address, and he, perhaps angered by my indifference, didn't ask for mine. He moved back to the States to finish a marketing degree at the University of Alabama. The next August, with no success in finding Dillon, I separated from the Army and pursued

{70}

a double major in religion and business administration at William and Mary. My junior year, I logged into my college e-mail account and found a message from Tyler Kossuth:

Done much dancing lately?

He had discovered my name in *Who's Who among Students in American Colleges and Universities* and found my e-mail address in William and Mary's online directory.

No, I haven't danced lately, but I miss it sometimes. I miss our driving to Maastricht on roads without telephone poles and electrical lines, with albino cows chewing their cud in the fields. I miss drinking chardonnay and licking it from your belly in the second story of the Belmont Hotel. I miss Christmas at the Bastille Opera House, the story of La Boheme, the yellow subtitles, and the long train trip from Paris, sleeping on your shoulder. I miss the delays. I miss so much about you, Tyler, but I don't miss you. I don't want anything to do with a lover who doesn't love me. Your appearance no longer controls me. I see you for who you are: an attractive man going through the motions of romance without the spirit. We had an opportunity to create our own methodology, to be unique and wise in our knowledge of each other, but you didn't care about that kind of dance. You wanted basic motions with simplistic people. I am not overly complicated, but I do need the elegance that comes with practice. Despite what I've experienced, I believe in progress in relationships. You may have had the talent to dance, but never the desire, and that makes you an amateur. As many things as I loved about you, I have no desire, now, to go through the motions of friendship. There is a part of me that hates you. I have no tolerance for a man who knows how to touch but not to feel.

Ava Brittin

I graduated from college without knowing what Tyler thought of my e-mail, but I assumed, since he never responded, that he had discarded me into that same barrel with all of his other minced romances. He had blended me into that compost of his dirty past along with withered bouquets, scraps of romantic dinners, and soiled prima cotton sheets. Burned and buried, I chose to remember him as the aggressor, the invader, the enemy from whom I had finally liberated myself. But, truth be told, there was no end to Tyler Kossuth.

Dear Ava,

I've spent the last four months in jail from a DUI conviction. At my request, my mother sent The Diary of Anne Frank. I've read it several times and thought of you so often that I started writing a journal. For the same reason that Anne Frank addressed her diary "Dear Kitty," each entry started with "Dear Ava." I guess I wanted to believe that I was writing an actual person, someone who would be with me regardless of how isolated I felt. Anyway, the Ava of my journal gradually became the Ava of my memory, and I began writing you, the only girl I knew who might appreciate the musings of a man who had converted to Catholic Judaism. If there is a part of you that hates me, then there must also be a part that doesn't. For the last four months, this journal has been my home. It's an extraordinary place hidden behind a plain facade. Within its halls, at the very center, is a ballroom. That's where you'll find me.
Tyler Kossuth

My Dearest Tyler,

I have inhabited your house each night (before sleep and

*dream) admiring the portraits on the walls, the pillars of the
golden mean, the frescos of a narrative that I wanted to be true
but that, in all probability, was fiction. So why do I feel genuine
again, wise for my patience rewarded? Why do I feel awash in a
happiness whose name is Good News? If joy is too intense, does
light have a broader spectrum? Does music have a stronger beat? My
life has changed so much since reading your journal. It's a holy
place. My nights are peaceful there. If I agree to meet you in the
ballroom, will you practice with me until we get it right? Or will
you threaten to leave should I step on your toes?*
Ava

Tyler and I married after several months of Sunday night
dance lessons. Sharing the same journal, we continued our habit of
expressing ourselves in words. We read what the other had written,
and responded as aptly as our hearts and talents allowed. In this
way, we each lived in the most intimate recesses of the other.
Sometimes, quite accidentally, one stepped on the other's toes.

{73}

*I haven't replied to your last three entries, Tyler, because I
haven't yet found a way to tell you what you already suspect. I
know that in this home of ours there is no hiding from the other.
For the sake of our marriage, I must invite you into a secret
place you did not know existed. Last week, when I went in for my
physical at the VA hospital, a man with prosthetic legs introduced
himself to me. A part of me didn't recognize him, but another part
did. His name is Dillon Snodgrass. Before I met you, he was my
husband. I suppose, technically, he still is. Much to my regret, I
accepted his invitation to dinner, and in the revelry of the wine
and reunion, I did the unconscionable. I have told Dillon repeat-
edly that it was an accident. I have told him I wasn't the type to
have an affair. He said I had been cheating on him for years. Ty-*

*ler, you know more than anyone that I am married to you in every
way conceivable. I can't explain why I went with Dillon, nor can
I excuse it, but please believe me when I say it will never, ever
happen again. I have never loved him as I have loved you. I hope,
in time, you can forgive me. I am sorry.*

Today is Memorial Day. The stock market is closed, the
confessionals are open, and this is the first entry of my new
journal. I'm a good Catholic Jew. We like to dig people up so we
can bury them properly. Quite the opposite of my husband, Dillon
Snodgrass is unaware. For instance, he doesn't know that I went
out dancing last night, as I do occasionally, meeting strange
men, hoping to find—what did Tyler say in his journal?—"spirit in
motion and love in life." More times than not, these men damage
me. As much as I would like to believe otherwise, my husbands
will never understand a woman who worships in two houses. I did
not intend to marry them both, but I was loyal to them both, and
for that I must live here for a while, until the war is over,
with you.

{74}

JILLIAN TOWNE
Herbes de Provence

in ten years, i don't want to speak english.
i want to wake breathing rosemary and lilies,
laced with salt from the mediterranean.

i want to wake up in aix-en-provence,
open my window to look out
on cézanne's mount saint victoire,
take my tea out to my white-iron balcony,
and dress to travel in to town to buy
thyme, baguette, and sweet crepes at
le grand marché, thumb through
first-edition leather covers walking through
marché aux livres on the first sunday of the month.

taking the tgv up through avignon and lyon,
i want to pass farms with fat cows and nubby shrubbery,
past les petits enfants running in fields,
chasing fairies and dandelion seeds. as the smoke
careens around the train and back toward the coast, i
will make my way toward la ville-lumière,
tripping over tenses and tongues
ordering les fleurs in the quartier latin,
order crème instead of sugar for my tea
in a clean, well-lighted place.

i want to spend the day at
jardin du luxembourg with my moleskin,
write lengthy poems about the nature of the flowers
and how they relate to champagne and wine;

{75}

write a novel about the way
french tastes in your throat on warm day
with a profiterole from la patisserie.
i want to write in intoxicating language,
with the lid off the blender,
excited to see what explodes.

i want to tango with his limbs in the quiet of the countryside,
listening to the waves crash
white sandy beaches singing songs of la mediterranee
as my own siren songs begin in my toes and make their way
up through wine stained lips. i want to give la bise
in the morning, a kiss on each cheek to keep the memory of me
like a fossil in flesh stone.

{76}

i want to dive into the fusion of france and italy
on the island of corsica; travel up north
through belgium, to see what the waffles are really like. i want
to run away on the monorail, and come home in the evening
to a bed that smells of lavender and a kitchen of herbes de
provence.

JiMMY J. PACK JR.

The Black-Drop of the Universe

This kid wore his high school football jacket every day no matter what the weather, a thick navy blue wool with white pleather arms and yellow letters sewn all over – DT / Ambler Football / Smith-Lineart. His first name was Alexander and he walked by every day, his headphones a set of clamped plastic laurels, avoiding eye contact, his head was lowered like a brontosaurus ready to feed. These guys are all the same.

And it was probably after the first month of passing me, while I was painting the railings of our apartment complex, when I looked into Alexander's eyes and, for once, he didn't lower his head and stare at the concrete. I don't know where my brain was for that month, not realizing an old curse I thought I (thank God) lost at eight years old had returned. Why didn't I see it in the way he avoided looking at me and dropped his as he walked by? I connected there, for a couple of seconds, and then he moved back into his routine – head down, eyes fixed on concrete. I realized he'd been wearing the same clothes every day and reeked of cigarette smoke and cat urine.

What I felt for that second lasted a lifetime in Alexander. And though I felt the emotions, I had only a few clues as to what caused them. That was when the high school football player transcended the seams of his jacket and those few seconds ate at me, they murdered that thing inside me, which helped me do the things I needed to do every day.

Three days after, the tenant who lived in the apartment next to Alexander and his mother was banging on my door demanding I go over and stop a fight. I tightened the belt on my jeans, pulled on a clean t-shirt and walked over. By the time I got to Alex's apartment the arguing stopped. Walking into the living room all

{77}

I could smell was the noxious odor of cat piss decaying hardwood floors, cigarettes smoked years ago and the tang of pot. Alex's mom was sitting in front of her computer talking to people in a chatroom – F4FPhilly – a glass of soda-and-something-else in her left hand with a More cigarette jutting between her fingers. She was small and fat, clad in a worn, blue flannel shirt and grey sweatpants decorated with stains of various shades.

"What? A mother can't discipline her child? Get the fuck out of here before I call the cops."

When she spoke you could see only one tooth left in her mouth.

I walked out without saying a word, closing the door behind me trying not to gag on the smell, wondering how she attracted anyone from any type of chatroom, let alone a lesbian chatroom. That explains all the women with overnight bags in and out of the house over the last few months.

{78}

I closed the door to my apartment and sat in my recliner for a few minutes soaking. This was how you raised a child – drug addict mom, no cash, eating spaghetti and canned tomato sauce for dinner every night, the stench of organic filth covering every room, hanging in the air like something waiting to die. This was a story repeated all over the country, the world, a cycle as natural to people as the cultivation of plants and harvest every year. This was part of the cycle of my job, my own life. Of course I'd seen this kind of mess before, but it was different this time.

I went to the fridge for a Miller High Life and that's when I went into that place, complete with my knees buckling and curling up on the kitchen floor in front of the cabinets under the sink. This was the place where the past kept itself tucked away in a synapse that was never supposed to go off again.

I'm eight years old. My parents, whose love had waned prior to my birth, decided to divorce. Mom leaves and my dad makes me sleep in bed with him to keep him company. As I listen to him cry

himself to sleep, I want to hug him, but I can't. Men aren't
supposed to weep. And when they mistakenly do, they do it in their
beds so the air is pushed out slowly through vocal chords that
don't vibrate; a whispered moan dissipating into the air and heat-
ing it with regret and loss. It scares me to see my dad so unsure.
I start to cry silently to myself.

And when dad is finished crying every night, he goes into the
world looking for someone to take his mind off the love for my
mother. He snorts coke with a girlfriend ten years younger than
himself and in the meantime forgets I am his son, so that at nine
I have to cook and keep the house clean and find his body stuck on
his bed, his sheets and pants stained with his dried urine, the
smell of feces and the sound of his joints cracking as I try to
move him.

I remember sitting on a creaky bed with a limp mattress in
the foster home of a family who takes me in for government money,
and I wonder if anyone will ever love me. And that's where I was,
alone in my apartment, watching the world go by – watching friends
marry and the seasons change, my skin getting a little baggier,
hairline retreating with some follicles gathering the gray rot of
time, aging me, wasting me.

I was sucked back into the now, imagining what Alexander
was going through – I felt it. Goddamn empathy. All that god-
damn feeling, and all I wanted to do was go to Alexander's house
and find him and just sit him down and hold onto him and rock him
back and forth until he was four again and maybe we could start
over. Maybe he could be a kid for a little while – maybe I'd go
to his football games and take him and his pals out to get ice
cream when the game was over. I'd take him to see an Eagles game
and buy him a hot dog; I could shove giant packages wrapped in
gold and red and green under the Christmas tree so, when he woke
up on Christmas morning, I could watch him open his presents and

{79}

then eat a turkey dinner. We'd have stuffing and mashed pota-
toes and chocolate pie and cold milk and a turkey carcass. And
then, in the summer, we'd go to the beach and I 'd worry as he
ran out into the water, watching his head go in and out of the
waves. We'd head home and sit in the backyard and watch the sky
for falling stars and he'd tell me his wish because mine was the
same, so it wasn't cheating. And I'd see him graduate high school
and feel so proud of the fact that he was ready to take on the
world, so smart and braver than anyone else. More brave than his
adoptive dad.

Even if we had to start at eighteen, I'd want to have him
hang out with his friends and come home at an indecent hour so
I could yell at him and tell him I'd been worried for the past
three hours and the thought of him getting killed by a drunk
driver was my worst nightmare. I wanted to worry about him as

{80}

he went on his first date with the woman he'd marry. I wanted to
see him graduate college and help send out his resumes, then help
him look for his first apartment and listen to him complain as
his fiancé was driving him crazy over the $3,000 price tag on the
flowers that will die anyway, and at the reception I'd tell him
how proud I was and he was the best son anyone could ever have
wanted, and as I hugged him I'd cry. I wanted to do something…
But all I could do was feel… until I finished a case of beer, like
every night, and passed out in my recliner. Yet another cycle
repeated all over the world.

The next day I was out replacing screen windows in the back
of Alexander's side of the building. He was walking home from
school and he stared in my eyes as he looked up to see what was
dangling out the second-story window.

I said, "Hey. What's up?"

Alexander stopped walking. He looked at me for a few seconds
and then snapped his headphones away from his ears and said,

"Hey."

    I smiled and he turned around, looked down to lose himself in the black-top of the parking lot with his headphones closing his ears. He headed back the way he came, and I went back to fixing the window, needing a beer.

{81}

JOHN SANDOVAL

Fond Memories

me and my girl
when we used to gargoyle hunt together
those were the days all right
those were the mornings that went as far as the eye could see
there on the shores of Cleveland Heights
there upon the banks of the Erie
not so very long ago, once upon a time
when she called me goat legs yet
(as I, upon a rock, with lewd tongue, took the night air)
(as she, Catholic lovely, exorcised blond, gathered shells in the dark)
those, sir, are the memories that are blessed indeed
when me and my girl, mischief makers twice   {82}
could make any dog bit bastard smile
and every one-legged waitress laugh
but now, somehow, all has gone passing
now, somewhere, upon the doldrums, we drift
(clever sailors ashore are not necessarily clever sailors at sea)
and in our rowboats separate, we tug bravely towards eternity
good deeds abandoned
Cleveland Heights in flames
there upon the waters of the Erie
neither one of us willing to offer
an oar to either one of us drowning

JOHN SANDOVAL
Frida Kahlo

black blooded Madonna hermana

crucifix penitante

catholic death embracer

Mexican heart coiled with barbed wire

Aztec dreamer of my dreams

magic mother of the dead fetus

Azatlan daughter

from one breast mescal

from the other tears

embracer of ugly giants and monkeys

redeemer of sins

forgiver of God

Jewess Mexicana bruja in the fire smiling

atop a pyramid stitching hearts

beneath cruel zia performing mass

beautiful hummingbird impaled upon a morphine cactus

twelve stations of the cross and you did each twice…

and then painted what you saw.

KATE DUVALL

The Twenty-Third Psalm For Rock 'N' Roll Junkies

The LORD is my shepherd; I shall not want.

He maketh me to bang my weary head against the flaming chainsaw
   guitar licks of the Sex Pistols; He leadeth me to cool the
   burn deep within the surrealist black-and-blue cosmos of Pink
   Floyd.

He restoreth my anarchist's heart and soul; He leadeth me in
   the paths of revolution against pollution, poverty, war,
   racism, disease, sexism, industrialization, globaliza
   tion, sexual repression, government oppression, and unscrupu
   lous recording-industry executives cheating thousands of
   musicians, singers, and songwriters out of millions of dol
   lars in due royalties for His sanity's sake.

Yea, though I slog through the barren teenage wasteland of the
   bubblegum pantheon of Britney Spears, the Jonas Brothers,
   and Miley Cyrus, I will fear no long-term brain-cell evapora
   tion, for Thou art with me; Thy barre chords and Thy backbeat
   they comfort me.

Thou preparest a Desert Island Jukebox before me in the pres
   ence of ever-increasingly and-alarmingly diluted FM radio and
   MTV playlists; Thou anointest my ears with the finest selection
   of buried treasures, deep cuts, and rare gems known to man
   kind; from Califone to Kraftwerk and from the Lime Spiders
   to Lyrics Born, my CD, LP, and cassette library runneth over!

Surely badness and coolness will follow me all of the days of
   my life, and I'll be the life of the house parties of the
   LORD forever!

{84}

KATHERINE AYARS
Like the Leg of a Y

The girl knows that he means what he says this time. She can
detect patterns and this morning, the pattern was different. This
is why she knows that today is the beginning of the good days.
Joseph usually says, "I love you. Don't leave." But this morning
he said, "I love you. *Forgive me.* Don't leave."

Forgive me. Yes, of course she forgives him. But she must
be careful. She must not change her routine just because he has
altered his.

She pads to the bathroom without a sound. It's as if waking
the dog will somehow alert Joseph. She opens the cabinet beneath
the sink and withdraws a writing tablet. It sits atop seventeen
others the same size. They're all full, every last
page decorated with her left-handed letters and numbers. As she
exits, she catches her reflection.

Her nightgown is old, but she refuses to part with it because
it reminds her of the first few weeks with Joseph. He had phoned
one day while she was ironing his teacher outfit, and he had said
that the vision of him and her living like man and wife had given
him an erection. Though she wasn't supposed to, she had gone out
that afternoon and spent twelve dollars. The pharmacy sold pretty
nightgowns in pastel colors and she had had her eye on one with
flowers and swirls; the design was soft and happy like a baby's
birthday cake. It was short, unlike her other nightgowns. She
never wore clothing cut too high or too low; she just wasn't that
way. But she had suspected the little housedress would please
Joseph. And it had.

The pen now rests more comfortably in her left hand than
it did at first. Four months ago she decided to train her brain
to think in a new way. She has read that right-handers use their

left brain and she wants to learn to use the right half instead – the half that the world's most innovative people use. Henry, who works at the store and sells her the pads of paper, says, "That's a bad idea." He says that she is charming the way she is and that she is in danger of changing her personality if she changes around her brain. Henry is old and wise because he has seen war, but she does not listen. She is a soldier with a clandestine mission, and she will see it through.

Joseph doesn't know about the eighteen pads, but he doesn't need to. Each day, as soon as he kisses her goodbye and closes the door, she practices her letters and numbers. She had a dream recently that told her to keep at it because the day she is able to form perfect figures is the day that Joseph will ask her to join him in matrimony. They will have a quaint outdoor ceremony. She will carry lilacs and wear no shoes and she will use her left hand to feed him a bite of cake while everyone watches. The guests will whisper that he is a lucky man. She will have a new last name and a newly developed brain and everything will be right in the world. But she is not in a hurry; rewiring one's mind is not a task one can accomplish overnight.

{86}

She doesn't have a job because, for a few years, she was in a relationship with a man who had a big fancy house and had asked her not to work. Not working her waitress job was fine with her because it made the man feel like a hero.

Joseph likewise wants to feel heroic, so he lets her stay home. And it's okay that his house is small and unsophisticated; she needs neither porcelain nor crown molding. The breakfast nook in this little house is flooded with sunshine and she can't think of a more perfect spot to build the dolls. She is crafting a collection that she hopes to sell in the general store. The dolls have special eyes. They're not those sneaky eyes that try to fol-low you around; they're eyes that look straight to one spot with a promise that won't be broken.

Beethoven's *Eroica* fills the room. She is proud that the
pattern has been carved into her brain but it hadn't been easy.
Joseph had yelled about her not being able to hear it, but as soon
as she had listened alone, it all made sense. Slow, slow, slow.
Fast, fast, fast, fast, fast, fast. She is embarrassed that it
took her a few listens to pick it up, but she knows that if she
does what he says, she'll be a better person. Like with the
shoes. Joseph taught her that taking them off without unlacing
them causes them to break down twice as quickly. He also made her
understand that vodka is cheaper than wine and that most people
can't smell it on you. Another bonus is that vodka doesn't make
you feel like you're still on a Ferris wheel the morning after.

A. B. C. One, two, three, four, five, six. Her hand doesn't
cramp like it did weeks ago; it's strong now. She fills every line
on seven pages because that's how many bites Joseph took to eat
his eggs and cheese toast this morning. Then she replaces the
pen's cap and looks in the pantry so that she can plan dinner.
He likes to eat chicken and cabbage and those tiny potatoes on
Tuesdays, but this Tuesday is not like the others. She wonders if
mixing up the menu will alert him to the change he has initiated;
she doesn't want to wreck things by creating too much variety.
She closes the pantry and takes the package of frozen thighs out
of the freezer. Then she washes her hands with scalding water and
soap.

She changes into pants and Joseph's old oxford and leashes
up the dog. Their neighborhood once seemed unfriendly, but that
was back when she lived alone. She used to like running into him
when she went on strolls. He found it endearing that she walked
even though she didn't have a dog, and she thought it was silly
that his black dog Buford had a white spot on his chest that was
way down low. It was as if his tuxedo jacket had been unbuttoned

{87}

after a long night of revelry.

The first time she ran into Joseph, she noticed that his pants were wrinkled and that they were too short. This convinced her that he did not have a wife. Or if he did, the wife did not know how to properly tend to a husband. When Joseph first told her his name, she said, "That's my favorite name. I've always known that if I have a son, I will call him Joseph."

"Don't laugh," he said, "but I find your name remarkable, too. I am a fan of the Russians and Anna is a name they often employ."

She didn't know what he meant by "the Russians," but she knew that he was smart. He was a music teacher at the high school. She couldn't imagine being so brainy that people would pay her to shape kids' minds. She had worked hard growing up but her father had realized early on that she wasn't made to be a surgeon or a lawyer or anything. He had encouraged her to work on her person-ality and pay close attention to her looks. She has this funny scar shaped like Greenland in her eyebrow and because her hair is dark and her skin is light, the scar is pronounced. This flaw has always bothered her father. He tells her it happened the time she fell out of her crib, but she thinks that story is boring. She imagines that as a child, a Greenlandic pixie branded her in the night because that's where she would settle with her husband. Her father had taken her to the make-up counter when she was young so that she could fill in the flaw. "You have to maximize your potential if you want to have a husband and appliances one day," her father had said. "Symmetry is important. It makes one look capable."

She was a very good listener and she had always listened to her father. But she stopped filling in the scar once she was on her own. She hadn't planned on it; it was just one of those changes that creeps up like a coffee stain in the kitchen sink. Slow and steady.

{88}

That's how her walks are. Slow and steady. She is patient
and now knows how to handle a big dog. She lets Buford lead her
to the right. This is the sign that he wants to go on a walk
she calls *I am with you*. She named it this because the pattern
involves walking straight into the sun on a slight incline, and,
being blessed by the ray's direct warmth reminds her that she is
not alone on this journey.

She stays out with Buford for twenty-nine minutes because
that's how old she is, then she heads up the front walk. She
loves walking the same straight line that Joseph walked only
four hours ago. She can feel his presence and she thinks she
can even make out his footprint.

When she moved into his home last year, he confessed that he
would return from their street corner encounters and think of her
while touching himself. She knows that some women might find this
degrading, but she finds it romantic, especially because her ex had
called that type of behavior "oddly voyeuristic." He was older
and very serious and had often said, "You should never do anything
you wouldn't do on the steps of a courthouse." She loved him a
great deal, but she had always had this feeling that she'd be lost
if he left her but found if she left him. She didn't want to live
her life on the steps of a courthouse. So, she packed her bags
and left him a note.

Buford loves returning from walks because it means that
it's time for a treat. She is allowed to give him only one even
though he would like to have two. She once gave him an extra and
that night he yacked all over the sofa. Joseph was so mad that
he hurled her hairbrush at the bathroom mirror. She was pretty
scared, but when it was all over she wasn't angry; she knew the
episode had occurred for a reason. The shattered mirror meant
that she wasn't seeing herself straight, and the brush's broken
handle was a sign that she should cut her hair like he had asked.

She washes up and gives Buford a biscuit. Then she reposi-
tions the pen in her left hand. Her letters are jittery, which is
not normal. She knows that this is because things are changing.
Things are wiggling and tangling and flipping all around. And as
soon as everything settles, she will be transformed; she will be
a blown-glass butterfly. Joseph will see how delicate she is, and
instead of dropping her, he'll place her high on the shelf among
his best records. She'll become a rare first edition — flawed but
beautiful.

She has forgotten most of the damaging words, but some things
won't go away.   This is the problem with loving a man who speaks
well; he knows how to say things like, "You are my sky, my all."
But he also knows how to say, "All you've ever done is keep a bil-
lionaire's bed warm." Her ex is far from being a billionaire, but
she knows that Joseph isn't great at math even though he's smart
enough to never end a sentence with a preposition. She also knows
that molding the minds of children requires heaps of patience and
sometimes Joseph is plain tapped-out by the time he arrives home.
Like what happened yesterday.

A co-worker had gone to Joseph's class to listen to the kids
play the violins and the clarinets and the cellos. After the mini
recital, the co-worker had taken Joseph into the hall and had told
him that kids aren't stupid; they can smell off-gas. The worker
had said, "You should consider having your last drink at six p.m.
instead of six a.m." The co-worker doesn't know that statements
like this make Joseph drink more than his usual share.

The extra vodka last night had inspired Joseph to carry a
kitchen chair into the garage and bash it against the wall until
his hands bled. She had listened to the destruction from the
safety of the kitchen and she had recited the alphabet from A to Z
and Z to A until it was all over. He had cleaned up the mess and
everything was fine. And he hadn't actually thrown anything except

{90}

words. Statements that didn't make sense and weren't directed
at anyone in particular. Statements like, "You don't know about
blood" and "All I remember is that there was a white dog."

When Joseph unleashes the gibberish, she doesn't say anything
back. This makes him even madder, but she doesn't have a choice.
Her mind just goes too dizzy to talk. It's as though the thoughts
are tumbling round and round in a dry cycle and all she can hear
is the loud "shhhhh" of the machine's exhaust. She knows that
sound is the world telling her to keep quiet and still. When
this happens, Joseph takes Buford out and after about an hour of
cooling down, he returns, showers, and climbs into bed.

Joseph likes to make love with the hall light on. She
doesn't understand why because he isn't able to look at her when
she's on top of him. "I have to close my eyes or I'll come."
This is what he says every time. She rocks back and forth for
a little while and whispers when she's ready. Then he opens his
eyes and stares at her breasts and they come together.

She slides writing tablet number eighteen back into the bath-
room cabinet and says, "This is just like making love. We will
now come together in new ways."

She sits at the table with her paints and basket of dolls
parts. The arms and legs and torsos are together on one side and
the heads are on the other. She fishes out a head with brown hair
and readies a paintbrush. She knows that this doll will have
green eyes because last night Joseph listened to Schubert's *Unfin-
ished*, one of his favorites. The number of letters in Schubert
is eight; and, in the case of evens, doll eyes are colored green.
When Joseph listens to someone with an odd number of letters in
his name, the eyes are blue. And when he listens to nothing at
all, the eyes are colored brown.

She blows on the doll eyes and sets the head down to dry.
She can't believe she has spent so long on this one pair; Joseph

will be home soon. She knows that things are different now. Better. But she wants to be sure. She must find a way for Joseph to tell her without words. She turns on the hot water and lets it run over the still-frozen chicken.   She thinks and waits and thinks some more.

Then she feels warm, so she showers. While she is soaping herself, she takes the empty cup from the shower caddy and fills it with water. She uses it to rinse the shower walls; he hates it when her stray hairs cling to the tile.

After she steps back into her clothes, she combs her hair with the brush that is now missing its handle. She thinks it's funny. The brush was once long like her hair, but now it is cropped like a bob. She has an idea. She will cut her hair. If Joseph notices the change before he pours his drink, then her suspicions will be confirmed; today will indeed mark the beginning of the good days. If he doesn't notice the cut until after the drink, then she will know that she has been wrong about it all. She will accept that she and he are a cloud that is pulling itself in opposite directions, and she will pack her bags and leave him a note.

{92}

She takes the scissors in her right hand and a clump of wet hair in her left. She closes her eyes then cuts. She knows that the dead cells can't feel, but *she* can. A row of miniature dominos lining her insides begins to topple. They start at her ankles and fall all the way up her spine. Faster and faster. Across her skull and down her arm bones. She opens her eyes and cuts. And cuts. And cuts.

Joseph was right; she does have a nice neck. She imagines that today he will come home and kiss it. He'll skip the drink and take her straight to the bedroom where they will come together like two raindrops that slide down a window and move into each other to form the leg of a Y.

She hears the door open. "Anna?" he says.

She rushes to greet him.

He kisses her forehead. "You showered. In the afternoon?"

"Yes. I don't know why," she says as she follows him into the kitchen. She knows her feet are moving; she can see them. But she can't feel anything except a scarf of air looping around her neck and shoulders.

He washes his hands and the steam fogs his glasses. It clears as he opens the freezer. She leans her hip against the counter for support. He removes the vodka bottle, the ice tray, then a glass. She runs her fingers down the back of her wet bob. He takes three cubes from the tray and anoints them with spirit. "You look happy," he says, "as if . . . "

"As if what?" she says as she leans harder into the counter.

"Tell me why you're smiling," he says, and he grins too.

"It's…"

"It's what?" he says. Then he takes a sip.

She slides her palm along the counter that she will never know after tonight and says, "Nothing. It's nothing at all."

KEN DiMAGGIO

Poem From the Spaghetti Scrapbooks (Cops)

Instead of a pin
your father's police
badge snapped the diaper
of what was even then
a trouble maker
--a joke your father
told you on every
birthday because like your
Dad his brothers and their
sons you were expected--

--but when the police officer
turned out to be your sister

--while her brother
got into more trouble
but now with books where
God was dead and Zara-somebody-
Nietzsche killed him

And if the police collared-men
of your tribe begrudgingly
approved of the daughter
badging into a man

was it because of the son
who did not believe in their
tradition of coffee donuts
& guns

--a boy who would never
wear a uniform

--a girl
who would never
be completely
accepted
for wearing one

{95}

M DELGUERCIO

Custody Suit

Except for demanding Sebastian,
Paulie was generous.
Her lawyer told her to give him the damn dog;
after all, she was getting the Golden.
Why did she want two dogs anyway?
Because she did.

"Can't we file a custody suit?"
Only Bunnie thought custardy suet;
and before the lawyer had a chance
to sabotage her strategy,
she conjured hard fat,
packed with cracked corn, suspended

from a branch for crows to peck at.
"Ms. Lapin, come-back-come-back-wherever-you are!"
"Promise him that I'll cook for him for a year."
"What?"
"Paulie will accept my offer. Trust me."
She served Chai tea with apple bran muffins.
"Are you crazy?"

"I want the dog. Paulie loves my cooking.
But he is responsible for delivery.
He pays food costs and $350
per week for my labor."
Without warning, he jumped her. "How good are you?"

"No!" Bunnie exploded. But then she did

what she promised herself she would never do.
She projected his body like a steer's
with all cuts of meat labeled.
"Good enough to know you'd make
lousy filet mignon."

And she flipped him, fuming,
"Get me my dog," all the while
rolling dough, fluting crust
for special mincemeat pies
as two Bengal tigers
approached expectantly.

{97}

MADDY HOPPERS
Living Arrangements

Our

downstairs

neighbors make such

a racket so early in the morning;

ringing and ringing then plopping and popping

dinging then whispering and yelling and clacking and slamming

Our

neighbors act like

they don't even know we are

there. They refer to us as rats, just 'cause they paid

more for the place, just 'cause their section is cleaner, fuller, bigger

and brighter.

{98}

When

the neighbors

leave the whole house grows

quiet, then sighs deeply and lets us sleep.

Then

we

eat.

Our

neighbors

don't know we have

access to their section. We would make

good house guests if they would bother

to invite us. We only take or use what is

necessary and try not to disturb any item.

The old dog waits for us to come in and is

thankful for the company and the scraps.

MADDY HOPPERS
The Red Socked, Black, Bully Cat

"Tell me a story."

"What?"

"Tell me a story. Any story."

"Umm. Will you just give me a second I'm thinking."

He began, "Well, there was this girl named Jen. I screwed the shit outta her last night. When she awoke refreshed in the morning, she was so thankful she went to go get me some delicious, frothy orange juice. She left naked and it was a rather crisp morning. She left right as the sun started to rise but the light felt cold, the way sometimes certain yellows feel cold when you know they should make you feel warm. Same with certain vibrant blues that feel hot, like the warmest part of a fire, closest to the burning, crackling wood."

"Well, you are in a strange mood this morning"

"Did you want a story or not? Why ask for one if you didn't want one?"

He continued, "On the back porch she met a big black cat, towering over a skinny white and grey dotted thing he had just gutted. He stared at her with his slatted orange and black, Halloween eyes and muttered, 'Get me some tuna and beans while you are out.' Then he paused and took a second to dip his paw in his prey then turned again to her,

'Bitch.' She made a wide birth around the cat and nodded her head, praying not to be the next gutting victim. She remembered she must return through the front so that she could evade the black, bully cat but she would buy the tuna and beans just in case. She skipped and skated down the slanted sidewalk. The rain had melted the sidewalks and the morning air had refrozen the

{99}

cement and it was slick and shimmering. She smiled and waved at
people on their porches and they smiled and waved back in uni-
son with heads cocked to the right and blank eyes. Even the dog,
who awkwardly lifted his paw but did not wave it back and forth
grinned wildly."

"This is just silly."

"What do you want from me?"

Again he continued, "She twirled and glided across the slick
cement and the yellow sun and the remnants of the Swiss cheese
moon twirled and skated over the slippery frozen horizon. In fact,
the moon is not Swiss cheese: it is in fact blue cheese, but
you have to actually be willing to give it time to realize. Her
nipples hardened in the cold yellow sun."

"Ok. That is not necessary."

"I'm just trying to tell the story—if you don't want to hear
it, leave."

He sighed, "A large crowd of fat, on-looking ravens lined
the telephone wires and made them sag low so that they were inches
from the ground. They told tales because they could, not because
anyone was bothering them to do so. And their stories were deli-
cious, dark, and deadly. They all told a different story, but ra-
vens can't listen so none of them pay any attention to each other.
That is why they are so mean spirited because no one listens who
could understand. Jen felt colder as she skated slowly past them,
with her head held low.

She tried hard not to listen, but they got in her head and
made her breath fast and made the fear rise through the shimmering
cold cement into her calves and, eventually, her lungs. The ravens
disliked her reaction, so one of them glided down and ripped off
the top of her head. She died and the melting cement sucked it
into itself as the sun warmed the earth and everything solid again
became liquid. She never brought me back any goddamn orange juice.

In fact, she was a bit of an idiot: even if she had made it to the store, she had not brought any money. Being naked and all made it hard to put cash anywhere. I went to the stove and cooked up some beans and tuna. The black bully cat clawed at the door, so I let him in. He grinned big and his red spotted, dentures shined. He told me what had happened to Jen, and I felt a little bad about thinking she was an idiot, but being dead really doesn't change what she was. He told me how he had found a weak raven who had sagged too low on the telephone wire, and forced it to tell him a story. He then painted each of his paws red. He stretched and stood up to put his caked, dark red, front paws on the stove top, looked up at me and laughed."

"I think I have to go."

"When you leave make sure to lock the door."

{101}

MARK GONZALEZ
Indefinite Sedative

He spoke sternly and was calm.
Walking through the hallway he
said it's probably completely
black, as the night sky without
stars, I thought. We
walked some more,
him thinking and
me wondering.

"Have you ever been out,
In the middle
of the ocean At night, the hushed
air around The boat,
slowly
you Look over the edge of the tiny
vessel. Nothing But black."

The void, I thought.
"The abyss" he said.

Staring at it, no reflection.
The stars are crumbs in a thick blanket.
clouds slowly lay across
the sky. It's darker now. Looking out
I pictured there to be more.
It was empty like the cookie
jar in a house full of kids.

Looking down into the water
My hopes are extinguished,
Replaced with fear. He says
            "That's probably how it will be."

{103}

MATT REEVY
Love Seat

My name is Melvin, and I like furniture. On a day I can't quite remember, I was left alone with my father's wood lathe, and there was no turning back. There's something about their curves, the way a nice piece of mahogany looks under candlelight with Louis Armstrong playing in the background... They're irresistible, these chairs, these tables, these living room accessories. So when it came time for me to make my way in the world, it seemed only natural that I would open up my own boutique, Melvin's Furniture.

People come into my shop when they want pieces crafted with love, tenderness, and passion. Each piece I create is completely one-of: handcrafted to fit the needs of the buyer as well as their personality. Of course, there are times when I can't bring myself to sell-sometimes pieces are just too gorgeous to let go, or they stun me with the force of their personality. Those end up in my private collection, and I refund the buyer's money and refer them to another shop in the area.

{104}

That was how I came to meet Ethel. Ethel was originally order #1129, a fairly plain high spindle-back made of maple.

The buyer probably would've left her in the corner of some kitchen somewhere and forgotten all about her; I knew better. Ethel was a hell of a chair underneath her plain, varnished exterior. She loved Coltrane and Beat Poetry, and when she first came out of my workshop I knew I had to have her.

"Ethel, would you like to come to dinner with me?"

Melvin... I don't know, I just met you. How do I know that you're not some kind of freak?

"I'm sorry, Ethel, I didn't mean to be so forward." We ended up ordering in. She got a nice bottle of teak oil, and I had a glass or two of my finest white wine. I don't remember what we had to eat, but I'll never forget making love to the sounds of <u>Giant Steps</u> on my record player.

After that night, things got a little awkward. I'm all for staying at home, but Ethel was a total shut-in. She never wanted to go anywhere, she didn't want me to work, all she wanted me to do was to stay at home and oil her up. But the sex was boring, too. One position only, and maybe if I was lucky I'd get to sit on her for a minute or two. She was definitely a conservative kitchen accessory.

But the orders kept coming in, and I was busy enough not to mind. For all her faults, Ethel was faithful, and she loved me in the way that only Spalted Maple Spindle-back can—I think its something in the grain. We had our rough patches, but with a little sandpaper and some understanding, we got by.

A month or two later, Dr. Stuhl came around to the shop. He was a regular customer, made all his money doing celebrity relationship counseling in the Eighties. He always wore his leather jacket into the shop, a gift from C.C. DeVille, the guitarist from Poison. Dr. Stuhl hadn't been able to save C.C.'s marriage, but he'd certainly saved the patent leather jacket.

"What're ya looking for today, Doctor?" I had the bottle of teak oil ready—Dr. Stuhl came around once a month to refill his supply.

"Melvin, I'm actually here to put in an order." He grinned at me.

"Really? That's great." I couldn't work up any enthusiasm, Ethel had stopped talking to me. She wanted me to stop smoking after we made love, told me she was sick of smelling like stale smoke.

"You don't look like you've been sleeping very much."

I shrugged.

"Let me guess, you're having trouble at home?"

"It's complicated." I said.

"Well, I guess I wouldn't be in any position to help. I didn't just retire from a successful counseling career or anything." He adjusted his leather jacket.

"I just don't think my workplace is really the right environment to talk about it."

"C'mon, we can talk. There's no one else in here." Looking around the dimly lit display floor, I saw he was right. I put the sign on the door saying I was out to lunch, and we sat down at the register.

"Well, uh, you know, she's a little plain, which was all right at first—but she's just not beautiful to me anymore." It felt great to get these feelings off my chest.

"So you think the honesty is leaving the relationship?"

"I'm not sure... Listen, I really don't feel like talking about it right now."

"That's fine, that's fine. Why don't the two of you swing by on Tuesday? Now that I'm retired, I've got a clean schedule."

"Yeah, I think we could do that."

"Great. So about my order..."

He wanted a chair for his den. 100% African Ebony, no expenses spared. This was a vanity project through and through. The work went quickly, and almost before I could blink Moaneek was finished. Ethel might have had a discreet charm, but Moaneek was a bombshell, all smooth curves and sloping, obtuse angles. She looked great, and she knew it. It didn't take long to fall head over heels for her, but I couldn't work up the courage to say anything.

Tuesday came around like a quick buyer, in and out before I could say anything about it.

I'm not going to any counselor!

"Ethel, please." This was the fifth time I'd brought up the

meeting with Stuhl. She hadn't budged yet.

No! We don't need anyone else telling us how to work. You just need to get away from your work a little more.

"Dr. Stuhl is a friend of mine, and I'm going over there with or without you."

Fine! You go! Go tell your friend you're fucking a chair!

"You're ashamed of me, aren't you?!" I didn't let her respond, slamming the office door on the way out.

Dr. Stuhl's place was exactly the kind of home you'd expect from a relationship counselor—lots of couches, lots of pillows; mostly neutral colors, although he had great taste in his furniture, even if he hadn't come to me for it.

"Melvin, nice of you to arrive. I thought we were going to have a group session?" Even inside his own home Dr. Stuhl didn't take off his leather jacket.

"Ethel was a little apprehensive about doing this." He lead me into one of his counseling rooms, where I got to cozy up with a lovely lounge sofa.

"I understand. The truth can be hard to handle." I watched him take out a pen and paper from his desk—a classy mahogany. "So you told me the other day that you were getting bored with her?"

"Its not just that. There's this other girl..."

"How original."

"She's a ten. Curves like you wouldn't believe. Normally I don't go for tattoos, but these are just so... gorgeous." I was thinking back to the raised inlays on Moaneek's back panel. Closing my eyes, I could almost feel the African Ebony under my fingertips.

"Right." Stuhl was scribbling like a maniac.

"And, I mean, there's sex problems too. With the plain girl. It seems sort of..."

"Unemotional?" Stuhl finished, his pen still flying across

Willard & Maple XV

the paper.

"Exactly."

"Well, this sounds pretty routine. Listen, I'll head by the shop on Thursday, you said my chair was done, right?"

"Yeah, she's ready to go whenever you want her."

"Fantastic." He showed me to the door. "Hope you get things sorted out."

I got back to the shop late, and I still had to put the finishing touches on Ben, an armchair for a recently redeployed Major. We talked a bit, Ben and I. Most of the time we talk politics, but tonight it was strictly gossip.

I heard Ethel wasn't too happy with your longer hours.

"She'll have to deal with it. I've got so many orders I can barely think. Is this enough teak oil?"

Yeah, that's plenty. But we know what's really been bothering you, Melvin.

{108}

"I've missed a spot, let me grab some more oil." I rushed to the counter, trying to keep my voice under control. "What do you mean, what's really bothering me?"

Moaneek.

That was it. They knew. All the chairs in the shop. Was I that obvious? What was I going to say to Ethel? The jig was up.

She said you were cute.

MATTHEW MCCAWLEY
Hot Tar

So much could be said
About the portly man who stands
Next to a busy road
In his pitted long sleeves, dirty blue jeans, and old
Work boots
With a sign that says

STOP

and SLOW

{109}

On a day when the sun
Beats down like a heavyweight fight
and toxic hot tar invades
Every receptor in your nose
Bud on your tongue

Is someone going to give him a bottle of water?

MICHAEL FULOP
When I Try to Imagine Your Death

It does not happen.
What happens is that you go on living
In the four rooms and kitchen of your apartment
Which allows a certain amount of freedom.
In this your husband, who is my father,
Chooses to join you.

In the half light of a perpetual morning
You and he sit at the dining room table.
I can see you drinking hot coffee
Or getting up to make fresh coffee.
I can see him reading the newspaper
Which is so thick that it must be Sunday.

Neither of you talks or thinks about
The infection which has persisted in your brain
For years but no longer has a meaning.
In the corner the cat cleans herself
A few hairs at a time with her pink tongue.
Now and then one of you watches her.

In a way, time passes and one summer
A bird flies into and out of your living room
Through the glass of the enormous window.
The next autumn you are almost happy
When the leaves blow through the walls of your apartment—
It has been so long since you could touch them.

{110}

MICHAEL S. MORRIS
Li-Po

Though one does not want to know —
I wonder of Li-Po, was he an itinerant
drunk who, raising his head from the
liquor bowl, would incite the stars
to dance on the water's surface like
cranes. What one does not want to know
about were the troubles, those malicious
conceits that sang on the one hand
of genius and left the other hand open
and empty and waiting for what poets
coin. Did he limp or stutter, was he
bald and stooped or could he carry
a barrel, a barrel full of spirits
in his youth? Or did he go the way
the imagination goes, finally realizing
his suffering he sang no more. Though
one does not care to know, about Li-Po.
About poets around a fire lifting their
glasses to the best in the poetry
contest, about this glowing gem
of a mind, there is a whole life
to imagine, as if his thoughts were leaven

{111}

PATIENCE HURLBURT-LAWTON

Meu Pai Com Olhos Verdes

My father is
Warm
Dark
Madeira in his blood, in his
Eyes
Green like pine, like
Chá verde.

He used to
Tap his Vic Furth drumsticks
On my knees
And sing
"Goodnight" to me
By The Beatles when I was
Falling asleep.

My father would
Dance with me in the kitchen
After ballet, or on
Sunday mornings

My father would
Crack open the door to my room
The light leaking through
And sit on my bed.
He would lean down and
Put his arms around me
Humming

"Good night
Sleep tight"
Strangers' cigarettes
The bitter backstage smell
And his musty jacket
Swimming into my
Dreams.

{113}

PETER LUDWIN
Observance

On the first day of hunting season
I watched you load the shells
into your .30-.30 and jam it
between us in your truck.
Then we drove the back roads
looking for bucks that had come
down to the hayfields to feed.

Alone in that golden ocean,
I thought you couldn't miss.
But we saw only three does.
Years ago you shot one
that refused to die right away.
You didn't want to relive that.

Besides, you had other game in mind.

The truck bounced up a dirt
track until we topped a ridge.
That's when I saw the grave.
The mound of flat rocks
Where you'd buried the ashes.
The ten years you'd shared.

Cranking up his favorite Dave Matthews tape,
you poured a beer over the stones.

I could see Wallowa Lake from that ridge.

The bones of Old Joseph, Chief Joseph's
father, lay under a monument there.
I wanted to put my arm around you,

a border too dangerous to cross.
While you picked some flowers
I sipped my own beer. In this
landscape of the dispossessed

tried in vain to fly.

{115}

RACHEL PALMATEER
Dead Man's Jacket

Lightning cracks the darkness outside your window
your ghost house is briefly illuminated
in shades of blue-grey, though the energy outside
strikes ice-white through the rain.
Not even the light in the fridge works and with the next flash
I'm there.
Locked door, locked windows…
Am I an apparition? How long have I been hiding here?
I know your thoughts.
It goes the same way every time.

I wear a dead man's jacket,
the blood on the collar never dries.
Don't worry, Darling,
it's not like I eat everybody.

First, I watch their lives play out,
like going to the theatre without
having to sit down or pay.

Like writing the screenplay
of every happy family
before the ugliness breaks loose
and turns a sitcom into a tragedy

Then, I get a little closer.
I sneak myself into their lives,
that face in the back of photographs
that you didn't notice before.

{116}

That kind foot snapping down
on a rolling quarter
necessary to complete your purchase.

I collect their scents,
shampoo on Mondays, sweat on Wednesday afternoons,
perfume Friday night while on the big date,
sex and his aftershave
while getting coffee the next morning, late for work.
I collect their schedules, grocery lists, missed phone calls.
I become a living scrapbook of their lives.

And then I wait.
The storms roll through
every couple of months, the perfect excuse
for the power to fail
and my teeth to grind in anticipation.

I once drooled on a man's couch
and had to burn it, him, his cat
in the dumpster outback.
The authorities thought lightning hit the thing.
I guess I'm a force of nature, too.

But you,
you don't need to fear me
because I don't know what cereal
you eat every Sunday morning
or when your grand mother passed away
or what color flowers you used at your wedding
because I don't know what name
you gave your miscarried child

or how old you were
the first time you had sex.
I'm not after you.

I just need to borrow some salt
for the roast I'll be cooking next door
when the power comes back on,
the one you say smells so good—
good enough to die for.

RACHEL PALMATEER

If You Are Like Me

Isaac Cruncher Speaks in the Community Room
at the Polk County Asylum for the Poor and Insane

If you are like me
you swallow hula hoops hoping
that a residue of human energy
is still attached.
If you are like me
you enjoy skipping skulls like throwing
elbows through windows
built of femurs with the marrow
sucked out.
If you are like me
you have signed up for the job
in the ivory castle, headquarters of
The Consumption of Life.
You will have built a piece of furniture
from the body of a wolf
for initiation, you will have
chewed your way through fields of Rhododendrons,
raising scarecrows for each flower felled,
jaws juicing every plant
like sucking blood.
If you are like me,
you understand that breathing creatures
were built to bleed, that souls
are gifts like chocolate covered cockroaches
meant to be sucked dry, drier, empty.
I climb trees to strangle squirrels and puncture

Robins' eggs with my thumbs
so that I can taste the screams of life
clinging to bodies.
I run my tongue over sidewalks
because humans once walked there
and I might taste a heel
through an over-worn shoe.
It's all about energy, you understand,
because the mountains have already swallowed
all the lightning
and the oceans ate the thunder
years ago.
If you are like me
you are a life lapper, an energy exorcist, a
cool calm and collected consumer, scavenger,
wearing the badge of Death and his determination
to clean up the mess that the gods made;
life scattered like broken crayons across their playground.
If you are like me
you were built with a hunger
that howls under your skin
and teaches you to make bricks out of bones
and throw them like stones into the ribcage
of coyotes and rabbits.
But if you are not
one of the open-mouthed open-eyed workers
I am counting to ten.
If you are here at the end of the numbers
if you are still here then,
you can scream monster, scream hate and hollow prayers
but nothing will save you from my savage hunger
and I will not give you the grace

of a game chase

I will laugh my teeth through the fur of your fear

and shake what you cling to

right out of your skull, I'll

build mansions for monarchs out of your body

and get a promotion

at the ivory castle, headquarters of

The Consumption of Life

I will thank you for living and swallow your spirit

and you will be grateful that I did it so swiftly.

But you will taste blood and banquets of flesh

at my promotional party

if you are like me.

{121}

RANDALL BROWN
As A Joke

He measured the fabric for awnings, cut the pieces, sent them to the sewing machines. They called him the wunderkid, how fast he picked it all up, how quickly he figured out angles, the unerring accuracy of each pencil mark, each cut. At lunch, one of the saleswomen took him to her cottage, put Delta Dawn on the record player, poured the Wild Turkey.

"You making her?" the owner would say to him when they were alone in the shop.

"Shade, man," he'd answer. "That's all I'm making here."

He reeked of independence.

When he left, she gave him a card, a tiny awning, complete with grommets and a note, "Good luck in Florida. From the 'Whole' Crew." When he'd come upon the card among yearbooks, half-filled notebooks, old report cards, even 8-tracks of Rush and REO Speedwagon, he couldn't recall much about the cottage, only that sometimes, as soon as he finished his cuts, she'd yell out "Cancel that order!"

RICHARD LUFTIG
Hunting Seasons

This angry autumn is almost gone,
taking what it wanted and leaving
what's left behind to fend for itself.
Soon the first bully winter winds will begin
to plunder the cottonwoods. It is almost

too easy for it to be a sporting game.
High overhead, a hawk's circles amidst
a late November sky, with his head, curved beak,
his talons protruding like the doors
in the belly of a bomber. He arches

{123}

above the crest of pinion pines and heads
across a neighbor's fallow field circling the dead
or dying stems and stalks of corn, hunting
for any field mice too recalcitrant to heed
winter's first veiled, half-hidden threats.

RICHARD LUFTIG

Speed Dating

I'll make this quick.
I get two minutes to make you
think this is not
about me when we know
this is all about me.
One minute to go
to not understate
or overreach, to put
my best foot forward
without sticking it
in my mouth or tripping
over my tongue.
Thirty seconds left
to try to keep you
interested, just enough
time (perhaps)
to tell you
that the most
important thing
you should know
about me
is

{124}

SKYLER LENDWAY
Halo

The world swam slowly back into view, blurry colors slowly defining themselves into objects and shapes. Allen blinked half-heartedly, rubbing his eyes. He could feel the new bump in the back of his head, accompanied by a dull ache.

"Good afternoon, Mr. Fredericks. Your operation went smoothly, and the healing has begun just fine." A small, slim woman in a pastel green uniform stepped into his field of vision. She leaned over him expectantly. "How are you feeling?"

Allen blinked again, groaning softly. "Like I've been drinking heavily. How long have I been under?"

"About 24-hours," replied the nurse. "Longer than most people, but not nearly long enough to cause concern." From the table beside the bed, the nurse produced a small hand mirror and handed it to him. "Would you like to see?"

Tentatively, Allen Fredericks lifted himself into a sitting position. Taking the mirror from the nurse, he lifted it to his face. There were all his usual features; nose, eyes, ears, all right where they should be. But there, hovering just above his head and emitting a soft, white glow, was the Halo. Allen turned his head to the side, inspecting the new lump on the back of his skull. "You can barely see the implant," he commented.

His nurse smiled. "People generally say that it feels larger than it actually is. Give it a couple of days to grow on you, and it won't feel nearly as foreign."

Allen nodded. "Is it functional?"

"The default settings are programed to self-boot as soon as your alpha-wave activity stabilizes. Now that you're awake and active, it should only be a matter of time." She turned her attention to the monitor set into the wall above the table. "I see no issues with any of the vitals that we're monitoring, so after a few simple motor function and mental aptitude tests, you're free to go. I've just notified your wife, so she should be here shortly. Oh, and you'll need these."

From the pocket of her uniform, the nurse produced a small, oblong plastic case. Allen took it from her, and opened it to find a pair of square spectacles. He chuckled to himself. "These are fantastic."

"Glad you like them. Not many people request such a retro style for their monitor."

Allen pushed the spectacles carefully onto his face. Throwing the covers aside, he swung his legs over the side of the bed and found the thin slippers provided by the hospital. "Right," he exclaimed, rising to his feet, "Let's begin." He turned to the nurse, who had suddenly become a deep shade of red.

"Perhaps... we could find you a robe first?"

Allen looked down at his naked self, then back to the nurse. "Yes, let's do that."

******

Half an hour later, Allen sat alone in the small waiting room of the hospital. He stared impatiently at the large, pastel-green crescent moon that adorned the wall across from him, and fiddled with the pamphlet in his hands, labeled *Getting to Know Your Halo.* That was just a codename, of course. Officially, the devise was known as a R.I.N.G., which stood for Robotic Information Network Go-between. In essence, it was a personal computer, set apart in the fact that it sported the very latest in Direct Neural Interface technology. The implant in the skull analyzed brain-wave patterns, translating them to the orbital server above his head, which in turn responded to the information, and projected its results on the personal monitor of the wearer. That was, if it ever activated.

They had given him all the information he needed: how to charge the module, how the colors of the Halo indicated the battery life, and every last hard command that he would ever need for overrides. The only thing they had forgotten to mention was what would happen if the module ever decided to activate. He opened the pamphlet again and flipped quickly through its pages for the tenth time, hoping there was something he might have mis-

Halo module number AG2157 is now activating.

Allen gave a small yelp, dropping the pamphlet. He looked wildly around the room, desperately trying to locate the source of the noise. Suddenly, there was a dull flash in front of his vision. It sizzled like snow on a monitor, then sharpened and organized, forming words in the air before him.

Please present name:

Realization dawned slowly on Allen, and his adrenaline reluctantly stopped spiking. Reaching for his face, he removed the glasses. The words went with it. He looked down at the lenses in his hands and sure enough, tiny blue letters stretched across them as if they were painted on. Feeling silly, Allen returned the spectacles to his face.

Please present name. The message reiterated itself, flashing twice.

"Allen Fredericks," he spoke aloud. The screen gave no response.

Allen Fredericks, he thought to himself. As the letters appeared in his mind they also appeared on the screen.

Allen Fredericks, confirmed. Writing registration....accessing citizen database hub...

The words slowly faded from his vision, but were immediately replaced by the voice once more. It spoke with the soft, plain female tones of most audio interfaces, carefully and eloquently enunciating each phrase.

Good afternoon, Mr. Fredericks, and congratulations on receiving an alpha generation Halo module. Because this is your first activation, the complementary tour of display settings will now begin. First is full interactive mode. Immediately, the lenses came alive with windows and charts, displaying calendars, weather reports, stock information, countless items.

Allen blinked in surprise. "Oh jeez! No, not that!"

For those interested primarily in research, we recommend passive query mode, which is presented in auditory access for the purposes of this tour. The waves of bombarding screens disappeared. *Please focus your vision on an object of your choice.*

Allen glanced briefly around the room, and quickly found the large, crescent moon symbol upon the wall. As he inspected it, a small green cross-hair appear on screen.

{128}

Moon, said the voice in his ear, *a celestial body that orbits a planet or larger body, which is called the 'primary'. As an icon, this depiction is an international symbol for healthcare, allowing for easy access to facilities, despite language barriers.* The cross-hair disappeared, and the voice continued.

Finally, for the more low-profile user, is independent activation mode. All facilities and information is accessible, but only when prompted by the user. As the voice spoke, a small menu appeared, scrolled quickly through a couple of options, then vanished. *Please select your preferred display setting.*

Better stick with the third one for now, Allen thought.

Choice accepted, replied the voice curtly. *For more specific prompts and activations, please refer to any information provided by your installing surgeon or roboticist.*

To Allen's left, a door slid open, and tall, brunette woman entered the room. As she caught sight of Allen, she paused. He smiled back, a goofy grin on his face.

"Oh, honey!" She exclaimed, "It's lovely!" She rushed over to him, throwing her arms around him in a hug.

"You really think it looks good?"

"It really does make you look like an angel," she whispered in his ear.

"Laura!" He immediately released from the hug, catching her by the shoulders. "We've been over this. The shape and illumination are for aesthetics only! What if the someone from The Ordinance caught you talking like that?"

"I'm sorry, Allen," she sighed. "It's just that some religious sect has been leaving graffiti in the parks district down the street again. I passed it on the way here, and I haven't been able to stop thinking about it."

"Don't worry," Allen smiled, "I'm sure they'll have it cleaned up in no time."

"You're probably right." She smiled back at him, and they embraced again. "We should be getting back now. I've got dinner waiting."

"Alright then."

They strolled arm in arm from the building, heading for the car.

"And to think," she said, "My man has an alpha generation Halo."

******

Laura pointed out the cross as they drove past it. Not that she needed to; even though several teams of Ordinance cleaning droids were already hard at work with high powered hoses, the large, white cross could still be seen staining several sections of a large stone wall. What words that were still readable said something to the effect of: God shall-......-Divine-........-for your sins! Repent! Allen shook his head sadly as they past. "Poor misguided people."

"It's amazing, really," Laura replied. "It must be, what,

sixty years since The Ordinance banned religion."

"Most of it, anyway. That," He indicated the cross, "I believe, is a Christian symbol. They managed to last a bit longer than the rest, so it's no surprise that they're the last bits of resistance."

"It's a very nice image, don't you think? Such a simple, clean shape."

"That may be so," Allen replied, "But it breeds nothing but conflict."

******

The brochure had warned about the attention a halo might attract. It had been an official Ordinance insert, stamped with an important looking seal. *Be aware that, while the module itself is* {130} *ascetically pleasing, it may cause slight confusion among the general public,* it warned. *Please take care to remain calm and casual, and remember that while new technology always generates skepticism, it will soon pass with familiarity.*

Allen had taken this to heart. For his ride to work he had adjusted the tint on his windows, and even though it was nicely sunny out, he had parked in the sub-complex to avoid walking through the open lot. The corridors of the Ordinance Department of Research and Technology were empty as Allen made his way down the hall to his office. He hoped he had beaten Sarah to work, so the element of surprise could at least be on his side. He stopped briefly to punch in the combo, ducked inside as the frosted glass doors slid open, and tapped the button again to close them tight. He paused to catch his breath, feeling rather silly. What was he running from? It wasn't like he had done anything wrong, but ... it was just different. Allen straightened up and turned, to find Sarah gawking at him from her desk.

For a moment, neither of them moved. Allen could feel his cheeks flushing, ever so slightly. Finally, it was Sarah who broke the silence. "It's pretty," she managed.

"Thanks," Allen replied, slowly. "The color means it's fully charged."

"Interesting," Sarah mused, dropping the packet of documents she had been holding onto her desk. She came around from behind the desk, barely taking her eyes off the halo. "Is it as amazing as they say?"

As she approached, a small green square appeared on Allen's lenses, framing Sarah's face. *Identify?*, the voice in his head asked. *Sure,* Allen thought. The square disappeared, and was replaced by a list of information. *Sarah Summers*, Allen read, *Biologist employed at the Ordinance Department of Research and Technology. Female, 32 years old.*

"Sarah, how old are you?" Allen asked.

Sarah peered at him. "I'm turning 27 in April, thank you very much. Why?"

"No reason," Allen smiled. "And yeah, it's working."

"What's that supposed to mean?"

"Nothing, nothing at all," Allen chuckled.

Sarah eyed him for a minute more, then shrugged before turning back to her desk. "Alright then. The new cross-breed gene samples are in from the farms, and suits want a full analysis."

"Alright, lets fire up the scopes."

******

At noon, there was a knock at the door. Allen opened it to reveal a tall, white-haired man, clad in a beige cover-all and thin, static-resistant gloves. His green eyes looked Allen up and down, caught sight of the halo, and smiled. The man looked back down to Allen, grinning ear to ear. "I couldn't resist any longer. I had to come see it."

Allen sighed and shook his head, feigning exasperation. "I was wondering when I was going to see you today, Matt." He turned back to Sarah. "I'm going to take lunch now. You want anything?"

She waved him away, not looking up from her microscope. "Grab some water for me if you get a chance."

"Will do."

Allen walked down to the cafeteria with Matt talking all the way. He listened absentmindedly as the engineer bubbled like a brook in spring, occasionally nodding to answer a question. Mathew Harper, senior Ordinance engineer/roboticist, had had his hands in the inner circle of the Halo's design committee. They had been friends and co-workers for years, and it was Matt who had nominated him for a Halo. They purchased sandwiches from a cafeteria kiosk, and moved towards the open-air seating area, Allen doing his best to avoid the crowds of interested stares. Matt chose a table near the edge of the third-floor balcony, and they both dug into their meals.

"So, how is it?"

"Oh, sorry?" Allen shook his head, regaining focus. Matt was all eyes across the table, chewing expectantly.

"Uh, it's great," he replied, reaching up to tap it with one finger. "It's amazing how much functionality you guys put in such a small module." He chuckled to himself. "But I can't say I'm really used to it yet."

"Microptic data storage, my friend. It's the wave of the future. And I wouldn't worry about it. I mean, you've got a Halo! People would kill to be you right now."

"That makes me feel much better, thanks," Allen shot back, rolling his eyes. He took another bite of his sandwich, chewing slowly before swallowing. "Matt, can I ask you something?"

"Shoot."

"Why a halo? Why such an obvious religious icon?"

Matt stopped mid-chew, looking up at Allen. He was quiet for a moment, and Allen could tell that he was mulling over his answer.

"How much do you know about the Bans?" Matt replied atlength.

"Not much," Allen admitted, "but I know they were put in place to protect us."

Matt leaned in closer. "That's just the thing of it. Hundreds of years ago when religion and the church were still young, it really wasn't dangerous. What's dangerous is the people who believe it."

"What?"

"Keep your voice down," Matt hushed him. He looked quickly around, but the balcony was mostly empty, except for a pair of women sharing a meal three tables over. Matt turned back to face Allen, his voice hushed. "There was a time once when religion wasn't just accepted, it was expected. The vast majority of the world was religious, and if you weren't, then you were, well...weird."

"But that's absurd! How could something so barbaric be so customary?"

"I told you, it was never the belief. Listen, when I was a lad, just before the Ordinance was formed, there was an institution called Sunday School, where kids went to learn what society thought they needed to about Christianity. They had this book, all full of stories and situations about it's conception, but they all shared a common idea: goodwill towards man."

"Alright," Allen chuckled, "Now I know you're messing with me. Goodwill in religion?"

"You should have seen it then, Allen. The artistry! The music! It wrapped the world in culture and united people like you wouldn't believe! But that's when the problems started. The stories weren't all that black and white, you see. They were symbolic, metaphorical, allusionary, whatever you want to call it. And the more people started thinking about it, the more interpretation it got. Anyone could pick up a story and start telling people what they thought it meant, and they were listened to."

"Listened to?"

"People believed them! Masses followed like sheep, believing anything that led to a happy ending. You know about the holy wars?"

"Huge conflicts created by religious disputes," Allen replied mechanically, "societies killing one another over superiority complexes."

"Exactly," Matt nodded, "but that's just what's recent. People have been fighting religious disputes for centuries before that. The Crusades, The Inquisition, The Holocaust, witch hunts; any of this ringing a bell?"

"Well...no," Allen admitted, "I've never heard of any of that."

Matt shook his head, sagely. "The Ordinance doesn't teach it any more. Hundreds of years of history, covered up."

"But that's no better than lying! They might as well be trying to write religion out of history!"

"But they're not. Think of it as . . . pruning the garden." Matt sat back in his chair, folding his arms across his chest. "We're not trying to pull out the roots, we're trying to make it look like it did before the parasites took hold. You are wearing a Halo because the Ordinance wants people to see what religion was, not what it became."

******

By the time Allen returned home, Laura was waiting in the foyer. She smiled, kissing his cheek. "Welcome home. How was your day?"

Allen removed his coat and hung it neatly in the closet, letting the door slide up and flush with the wall behind him. "It was . . . enlightening," he managed.

"Well good! Listen, Michael just got back from staying with my father. They're both in the back yard, and John is staying for dinner." She smiled again. "I haven't told them the good news yet. You should go surprise them!"

"I really hope your father likes this," Allen muttered as they crossed into the kitchen. "He never seems to approve of anything I do."

"Come on, now, you know he never really got used to the rise of The Ordinance. But how can he not approve; you're one of the first people in the world to get a Halo!"

They stopped at a pair of French doors, leading out to the patio. In the back yard, Michael Fredericks could be seen playing catch with a small dog, while his grandfather sat watching from the steps. Laura opened both doors wide, stepping out into the afternoon shade.

"We're back guys, and do we have a surprise for you!"

Michael looked up from the dog. His eye grew wide, and his jaw even dropped a little. "Wow, Dad, that's amazing!"

From his seat on the steps, John Anderson turned to see the couple. Immediately, his brow furrowed. His eyes went icy cold, and despite himself, Allen shivered.

"What the fuck is that!" demanded John, rising to his feet. "What the fuck do you think you're doing?"

"Dad!" Laura protested, "Not in front of Michael!"

"You get inside!" he shouted back at her. "Take Michael with you!"

Michael now stood staring at the conflict on the deck. "What's happening?"

He sounded scared.

"Michael," Laura said sternly, "Come here."

Slowly, Michael came. Laura took him by the wrist, and, shooting a final angry look at her father, led him quickly inside. Once they had gone, John rounded again.

"What the fuck is that on your head!" He was already starting to go purple in the face, with tiny blood vessels defining themselves against his skin.

"Calm down, John. It's called a R.I.N.G., a Robotic Info-"

"Don't you bullshit me! That's a goddamn halo!"

Allen blinked in surprise. "Well, yes, but how did you know?"

John wasn't listening. "What gives you the right to wear a halo, huh? Who do you fucking think you are!"

"Hey, it was given to me-" Allen trailed off mid sentence. Realization was dawning again. "Wait, what do you mean?"

"Ha! You know exactly what I mean! You're all hypocrites, the lot of you! You and your stinking Ordinance! Wasn't enough to take our God from us? You had to go and take the halo off his head?"

{136}

"Careful John, you're making it sound like you're a Christian!"

John smiled a terrifying smile. "That's because I am." Grabbing at his thin button-down shirt, he tore at the material, ripping seams and giving way to bare skin. Clearly exposed on his left breast was a pure golden tattoo of a cross, with the letters INRI etched in under it.

Allen started in horror at the marks. "John . . . what have you done to yourself?" He looked back up at the older man, but John's face was now a mask of terror, eyes locked on the Halo.

"What?" Allen asked. He turned to his reflection in the glass behind him, and gasped. The module had begun to glow a violent red, and was pulsing steadily. Once again, the voice in Allen's head spoke.

Warning! Subject has been identified as religious sect member. Subject should be considered hostile and unpredictable. Module AG2157 is now contacting Ordinance authorities. Please remove yourself from the vicinity and seek shelter.

Suddenly, there was a hand on his shoulder, and he was being turned forcefully back towards John.

"What's going on?" he demanded, "What is it doing?" Somewhere in the distance, a siren started to wail, then began slowly increasing in volume. John's face went pale, all of the purple that was there a second ago now gone completely. "I have to go," he stammered quietly. "I have to get out of here."

"John, wait-" Allen tired to grab his shoulder, but John brushed him aside.

"You will burn for your sins," he spat. "You and all your ilk will burn for this." With that, he turned and ran, crossing from yard to yard, and out onto the sidewalk. At that moment, an Ordinance guard cruiser came speeding around the corner, siren blaring into full volume. As it turned, a small hatch slid open on the side of the chrome exterior. Allen couldn't see what it shot, but John froze mid-step and fell to the ground, shaking violently. People were beginning to emerge from their homes, peering warily out at the scene. From behind him, Allen could hear the stifled sobs of Laura through the thin glass.

"Our F-Father, who a-a-art in H-Heaven!"

John had begun to yell, stammering wildly as he fought to control his body. The cruiser came to a swift stop next to him, and from several side hatches appeared four Ordinators, dressed smartly in sleek silver uniforms.

"Hallowed b-be thy N-Name! Thy k-k-kingdom come, th-thy will b-be d-done, on Ear-"

One of the Ordinators delivered a swift kick to the helpless man, who immediately fell silent. Without a sound, the four enforcers gathered John into the cab of the cruiser. The hatches slid shut, and the vehicle quickly sped away.

This is an important message, broadcast from Ordinance authorities. The rogue religious sect member has been apprehended, and the state of emergency has passed. Please feel free to resume any previous routines. Repeat, the state of emergency has passed. Thank you.

STEVE BENSON
The Big Can Theory

"... like a melody you heard from the flowers when you were
three years old but forgot
          to tell anyone."   -- Diane Frank

Walking with my daughter she said:
"Jesus doesn't have to eat anymore."

"Is he on a new diet like Mommy?"
Her frown looked like her mother's.
So I quickly added: "Why doesn't he eat?"

{139} She patiently explained. "Jesus puts stones in a big can
with rain and dirt and stirs it all up until it's yummy."

She looked at my face to see if I was getting it.
Apparently I wasn't. Before I could stop my tongue I heard
it say: "Then you must favor the Big Can Theory of Salvation."

She peered into the red throat of a yellow-tongued tulip.
"You think flowers don't talk Daddy, but they do."

She looked at me and I was in both of her eyes.
"What do they say Sweetheart?"
"They want you to dig up your Daddy's bones
and hold them and kiss them forever."

Needing time to shake the Etch-A-Sketch in my head
until it was smoothly gray again, I looked up at three
dark pines pointing to hazy rows of crisscrossing clouds.

When I was able to see only one daughter again,
I asked her what else flowers said.
"Every time they open their pretty mouths they say something.
Everybody knows that don't they Daddy?"

But I still wasn't convinced. "What happens if no one
is listening?" She smiled and squeezed my big mitt of a hand.

"They spill their words on the ground. then the sun
sucks them up and they all fall down when it rains
so Jesus can scoop them into a tin can with some good dirt."

She dropped my hand and ran to an empty swing where I pushed her
gently at first, then faster and higher until she screamed.   {140}

SUSAN H. MAURER

A.A. 12-23-04

I came because you could not come here, Judith.
I wonder how it happened. I think slow.
I think you bought the best, drank quite slowly,
each sip quiet 'til you slept. Awoke and then began again
and again until you didn't wake. Wonder if there was a cat.

I can see you turn your nose at this grim room,
assortment of livers, stories of
living, interrupted by rumbling subways,
not always the best prose.

{141} Judy, the room has streaked linoleum. I'll describe it,
a basement without windows, questionable if mice sometimes…
I guess the Etruscan vase was your witness as you went, you slid.
Nothing seemed tasty enough to keep you alive.
This is your wake my golden friend. A.A. was not the only answer,
Judy.
But nothing good enough, you turned away. We failed.

SUSANNA RICH
Re: My Mother's Parole

Legal Counsel: "Your Honor, I am
not my mother. (for the record,

the defendant is whispering this prison
metaphor (not my fault), her conceit

to monopolize here.) . her crimes?
Many. Plagiarist. Copy-cat. She kidnaps

my words, repeats them to others, as if I
were a baby only she could translate

—echoes me, even to my husband,
my husband-she's perping larcenies

for his attention-limps to take his arm,
all gooey-dewy for wine. It's only payback

she thinks-when I was sixteen she madam-ed
me to her old boyfriends, to enthrall

them to her-her way, to sheathe
me in her slips, wrap my thighs in her

garters, remind me I am her
accessory, then blame me for stealing

men from her. Whatever I do or am,
she batters me to do better, other,

else-anything that'll make me into
who she is: not herself. Mostly she's guilty of

negligence-her sting to keep me gagged.
She's in lockdown in my body,

running her tin cup along the bars
of my sleep, Swiss-cheesing my dreams.

She sues me with frivolous suits-perjures
herself-claims elder abuse. She's thieved

{143} me of my trust that I can enable enough
love. She'll work her embraceries on you,

too. Too much solitary with her-not
separate enough for togetherness.

Your honor-parole her, please-this is self-
defense.can't harbor..." Advocate freezes.

Defendant crosses her hands into a Virgin Mary
on her chest. Weeps perjury-the poet taking liberty.

SUSANNA RICH
To Sperm Lost

Ejaculate of solo showers,
afloat in condoms, stewing in sewers

or spermicidal clots, stuck
in an ovum released too soon—

you, too, are at the dance
of the Universal Gym—

but staggered against some wall—
a misplaced comma, a tail

without legs to be between.
No one campaigns for you or

the eggs—all wall-eyed and stuck
against chairs, while the coupled marathon

on the floor of life—entangled in their
genetic symbioses, their first date—

their last—no long engagements, no
navigating a ring, no honey-anything.

But oh you, roadkilled en route to Eden,
your right to wife never to come . . .

{144}

T. M. BEMIS

Ground Zero

God was after Grover Prue. The young man knew that fact sure
as he knew his own name, though he couldn't have told you why.
He'd gone out of his way to be a decent fellow always; loyal to
his friends, respectful of his elders, pious and hard-working and
patriotic as the next lad—or no, much *more so* than the next lad,
he'd seen to that. Scrupulously. Altar boy, Eagle Scout, Honor
Society, he'd done it all. Yet the *Big Guy* was still out for his
hide, and no mistake. Grover had never actually discussed this
fact with anyone—at least not in so many words—but they knew it
too. His parents, his brother and sister, his classmates and even
the neighbors knew it. Because they'd witnessed, as he had, the
wrath in all its fury.

They'd been there, some of them, at the birthday picnic when
Grover turned six and the oak came down. A mammoth of a thing
it was: eighty feet high, old as the Colonies and solid as a
mountain. Or so it had seemed. In reality, it was hollow as a
gourd from generations of termites having their own picnic, and
down it dropped into the yard that day—square across the redwood
table where they were eating lunch. Grover's sister Rosemary
had just gotten up to play horseshoes, joined by brother Ralph,
cousin Clarence and Grover's three best buddies Philip and Seton
and Carl. Only the birthday boy himself remained on the bench,
polishing off a second slice of mocha-frosted birthday cake,
content as a clam. It missed him, that tree did, by about a yard,
guillotining the last two feet off the table like it were made of
balsa wood and pounding terra firma hard enough to rattle windows
in the houses nearby. Limbs had bashed around the boy with the
force of a hundred Louisville Sluggers, annihilating plates and
glasses and launching silverware in every direction, but sparing

{145}

the little redhead who popped up through the leaves, goggle-eyed and still chewing. A couple of years went by, and the oak-tree incident entered the realm of Prue family lore, embellished by each retelling until it had become a go-to anecdote to share with visitors and friends—their own truly astounding, once in a lifetime phenomenon.

Then the boiler blew. It was a steam explosion, the principal told them. The principal of Toddville Elementary School, that is, who admitted to Grover's parents that he was only repeating what the state inspector had explained to *him*. It seemed that the boiler's automatic feed water valve had failed in the closed position and let the drum go dry, but the safety switch hadn't shut off the fire like it was supposed to do when that happened. So the drum had gotten hotter and hotter until it was red-hot and

{146}

glowing, like the filament in a toaster. Only this was a steel tank twelve feet long and heavy as a Cadillac Eldorado. Then the valve opened again and let in the water—which flashed to steam so fast the pressure blew the thing apart like a popped balloon. It demolished a wall of the boys' lavatory next door, filling the air with deadly bricks and shrapnel. Fortunately, the room was empty at the time save for a lone occupant: Grover Prue. The second-grader had been balancing a wooden bathroom pass on an index finger and contemplating life from the perspective of the third stall when all hell broke loose. His life was spared by a sturdy metal partition which had absorbed the impact of the flying debris but not, alas, the accompanying sound waves, which had left the boy deaf to the world for nearly a week.

While inexpressibly grateful for their son's good fortune, George and Edna Prue couldn't
help noting the odd coincidence of a second, ultra-close call. Sideward glances were inevitably exchanged when the two events

were linked in conversation. But they got over it soon enough,
and Grover and his siblings went back to their studies, George
back to the photo counter at Q-Mart, and mother Edna back to
managing it all.

The following June, the family made its annual sojourn to
Happy Valley Amusement Land. It was a small park by modern
standards—one of the nation's oldest, in fact—and was home, there-
fore, to no supersonic theme rides, parachute plunges, curlicue
water slides or ersatz African savannahs haunted by geriatric,
kibble-fed tigers like some of its competitors. What it offered
instead was a charming, hand-tooled hominess that had endeared it
to generations of local families, and the Prues were among its
loyal devotees. This was one outing that even the elder children
needed no prodding to attend.

On line at the food stand, Grover was peering this way and
that at the wonderful and familiar sights all around him when
his gaze alighted upon a teenage girl by the entrance to the fun
house, who seemed to be staring at him. Too young yet to have the
social wares to make him look away, he had simply stared back, and
it was she who, with a tentative smile of embarrassed acknowledge-
ment, finally broke off their visual engagement. Only then did he
realize how charming she was, this long haired, fresh-faced blonde
in blue jeans and a sky-blue tee shirt, and the terrible crush he
would have on her that was even then taking nascent form in his
subconscious mind would be his first. He followed the gleam of
sunlight reflected from her hair until she was lost in a crush of
patrons entering the attraction.

After lunch, Rosemary and Ralph made straight for the Dragon
Coaster, while Mom and Dad escorted their little brother to his
own favorite ride: Spinning Sammy Spider. Lagging a few yards
behind them as he munched on a corn dog, Grover was approach-
ing the lovable giant of a whirling red bug, his eyes wide with

excitement, when it decided to come to him instead. With a hor-
rific groan a critical linkage let go, and one of Sammy's legs–a
twenty foot assembly complete with a two-seater car attached to
one end–broke free and sailed through the air like the hammer of
Thor. Mother Edna, turning at that instant to check on her son,
was numb struck: there was no time to reach him, to yank him from
harm's way, to do anything save give voice to the heart-wrenching
cry that ripped from her lungs. Grover didn't hear it. The
music of the calliope, the whoops and bells from the other rides,
the buzz of the folks around him–all of it was gone now as he
watched a slow motion, 3-D drama in rapt silence. The spider leg
was coming for him. Not to the right and not to the left, but
for him, Grover, star of his own disaster film. And he was rigid,
ossified, as fixed to the spot as if he'd been planted there,
watered and nurtured for nine full years in preparation for this
very moment. He watched the thing grow huge, until he could
plainly see two grownup faces over the rim of the car, a man and
a woman, mouths shaped in screaming O's, hair flying wildly as
they hurtled his way. Grover closed his eyes and sound returned:
shrieks and shouts and then a rush of wind and a terrible,
protracted crash–

{148}

   His mother seized hold of him now and spun him around to
face her, and when he opened his eyes he was looking at the tick-
et booth over her shoulder–or what remained of it. The roof of
the octagonal structure had been neatly shorn off, the supporting
uprights left probing empty space like an inverted stool. Beyond
that, he saw, Sammy's appendage had punched a hole straight
through the wall of the penny arcade, leaving a ragged silhou-
ette of itself before landing in a haymow at the Children's Zoo.
People picked their way through squawking chickens and bleating
goats toward the hapless couple still strapped in the car, look-
ing about as bewildered as if they'd arrived on the moon.

Grover's mother clutched him to her breast. "Oh, honey, *honey,*" she sobbed. "I thought
we'd lost you. I thought my baby was gone for sure." She thrust him away for a better view.
"Why, it came so—" Her eyes rose to a scratch on her son's fore-head, a scratch that led to a
perfect part in his hair that hadn't been there before, coincid-ing, she would find later, with a six-inch bolt distending dagger-like from the belly of the two-seater car.   "So *close*," she finished saying, her voice trailing off to a whisper, and George was there to catch her when she fell.

******

{149}   Life continued normally for Grover after that—if playing dodge ball with the Grim Reaper is what you consider normal.
When he was twelve, for example, lightning struck the aluminum flagpole in front of Toddville Middle School. The freak discharge of a single scudding cloud, no one was anywhere near the thing at the time—except for Master Grover Prue, who had only just turned his back on the shaft after having affixed a wad of chewing gum thereon in a milquetoast display of pre-pubescent rebellion. The pole itself survived intact, but Old Glory, vigorously awave be-neath a brass eagle finial, had burst into flame like it was doused with gasoline. As did Grover—or more accurately, his green flannel shirt—a nigh disaster averted by the quick-witted janitor, who tackled the sprinting torch within seconds of immolation.
Grover's injuries were thus limited to the loss of a favorite garment, and the embarrassment of sporting a mushroom-style coif-fure a decade or so before they came into fashion.
      Nobody thought that the boy was to blame. Anymore than they had when the Wawkatinny Creek Bridge collapsed a heartbeat after

his skateboard trundled across it; or a few months later when
the only recorded twister in Wooster County leveled the Captain
Cone Ice-cream Hut just as Grover tooled past on his three-speed
Raleigh; or a year subsequent to that when the façade of the old
Brewster Building had crumbled inexplicably into the center of
Main Street, pulverizing a Plexiglas taxi stand and a polka dot
VW beetle—but leaving the teenager poised between them unscathed.
Increasingly however, the townsfolk—and eventually also Grover's
own friends and relatives—began to keep their distance. It
seemed evident that even the most providential stretch of luck
was bound to run out, and that when it did, it would be the boy
proper rather than the surrounding acreage who would get clob-
bered by that particular sling or arrow of outrageous fortune.
Grover seemed to sense this also. Against the vociferous
protests of his parents and the enthusiastic recommendations of
his guidance counselor, he decided to eschew college altogether,
taking instead, upon graduation from high school, a caretaker's
position in a nearby town. By his estimation, this particular
job was ideal for his special needs. The salary wasn't the
highest, but it afforded him clean work and a place to live in a
community where the bus wouldn't empty out every time he climbed
aboard. But more important, this solitary calling allowed for
most of his hours to be spent atop a riding mower cruising the
spacious lawn, or at work in one of the gardens, or mending
fences in some remote corner of the estate, where he might be
spared the necessity of dragging others along with him on his
inevitable junket to the Pearly Gates.

And so it was that Grover, a troubled young man of nine-
teen, who felt in his heart as if he had already lived far more
than those meager calendar years would suggest, at last found a
measure of peace in his life. Not a peace that you or I would
appreciate, perhaps—what with rabid skunks waddling into his

{150}

path and the chain saw kicking back to trim his sideburns with near-metronomic regularity—but peace enough for Grover Prue. In the evening when his chores were done, Grover would settle into his little cottage to enjoy a frozen dinner and an hour or two of television. He was especially fond of the nature and history shows, where a discussion of the wombat's will to survive or a segment on the curse of King Tut's Tomb would strike a sympathetic chord. Later on, after the screen went dark and he lay awake listening to the mockingbird that flung its rejection of circadian rhythms so boldly into the restless night, the doubts would come. That dreadful introspection, when he'd wonder for the zillionth time if he had done something very wrong to bring this all about. If so, he would conclude, he sure couldn't put his finger on it.

And next, much as he tried to steer his mind toward the upcoming day's labor, or current events, or wombats, or anything else whatsoever, he would inevitably end up thinking about how it would happen. Which particular sweep of the scythe would finally find its target. Weird as it seemed, he didn't really dread the idea as he once had, didn't waste his time anymore on elaborate schemes of avoidance or escape. What was that saying that the alcoholics used? He had been granted the serenity to accept what he couldn't even begin to fathom, much less change. Death came to everyone sooner or later. For him, the scale was leaning a little toward the sooner side, that's all. He only hoped that it wouldn't be too painful when it did arrive, and he'd pray for that as his eyes drifted shut.

******

Grover dog-eared his paycheck as he stood in line at the bank. It was a Friday afternoon, and he was thrilled about a movie he'd rented to watch that evening. An action-adventure release, it was said to be chockablock full of the car chases, fist fights and outrageous shootouts that brought him such unadulterated joy. There was something in the sheer *phoniness* of all that Hollywood mayhem that he found incongruously soothing—even though, for obvious reasons, he wouldn't have touched a *real* firearm with a pair of tongs. Like that one there, he pondered absently. Darned if that didn't look just like the butt end of a handgun nestled inside the folded shopping bag under that man's arm. The fidgety guy with the unkempt, salt-and-pepper beard. But no sooner had this bizarre concept begun to crystallize than that very same stranger took a long stride forward away from the queue, and turned to address the others. Sure enough, his shopping bag gave birth to a nickel-plated revolver.

"Everybody down on the floor!" he bellowed. "This is a stickup!" Breaths were drawn in sibilant harmony by the dozen or so startled customers. Immediately they endeavored to comply, the younger ones with pliant ease, and the senior contingent in gradual, step-by-step progressions. "Hurry up!" he barked at a gray-haired lady midway back, and the smallest whimper escaped her before her husband, with a touch on the arm and a tight shake of the head, convinced his bride to stifle it. Taking her hand, he helped her descend carefully to the white marble surface, then added his own arthritically-challenged bulk to the prostrate congregation.

Apparently satisfied, the thief marched over to the nearest teller's window and shoved his paper bag through a slot at the bottom. "Fill this up with small bills, P.D.Q.," he directed. "And don't go pushing any alarm buttons, if you know what's good for you." A grim-looking woman with half-moon glasses opened her cash drawer, and began transferring banded sheaves of tens and twenties as instructed. For Grover, sprawled on the floor with his fellow patrons, the entire universe had been reduced

{152}

to the evil glint of that silvery pistol, not aiming at them now but angled insouciantly off to one side, as if to belie its lethal intent. He was so focused upon it, in fact, that he didn't notice that the customer next to him, a ruddy-faced gentleman in a dark blue blazer, was coiling himself furtively into position to spring. At the moment the teller unlatched her window flap to pass back the loot, this man leapt to his feet with the grace of a cat, brandishing a glistening weapon of his own.

"Police!" he announced. "Drop the gun!" There was a reprise of sucked breaths from the captive audience. Eyes on the bulging bag in front of him at the counter, the robber regarded it a beat longer—then swung about on the balls of his feet. He didn't stand a chance. With the safety off at point blank range, the officer merely squeezed his trigger. The resultant *click* was loud as a church bell in the absolute quiet: the gun had misfired.

Assuming himself a goner, the crook had screwed up his features in bleak anticipation, not even attempting to shoot back. Now, however, in the unexpected interval of continued health he gradually unwound, letting one eye sneak open, and then the other. It was not the detective's day. As he worked the slide on his automatic to eject the dead round he managed to jam the next one, so that he currently wrestled with a broken tool as intimidating as a bar of soap. Registering this misfortune, a sea change in attitude swept over his opponent. The man recovered his bravado, drew himself up to full height, and made a show of leveling his revolver with exquisite deliberation.

A notion arose like a bubble through the ice water of Grover's fear. When it reached the surface and burst into clarity, he did not hesitate. He was up in a flash and darting in front of the policeman just as the blackguard opened fire. A shot boomed out and then another, and again and again and again, each detonation deafening in the stone-veneered enclosure. To Grover's left,

a rack of credit card applications exploded into pieces. To his
right, a cardboard salesman hawking car loans was decapitated and
collapsed. Over his shoulder, a windowpane vanished to shards
and an instant later its neighbor followed suit. Directly behind
him, the policeman grunted with each report like a boxer taking
a punch. And then the banging ceased altogether as the revolver
went empty. The robber glared down aghast at the smoking gun in
his hand, and up at an unharmed Grover in disbelief. Several
seconds passed when no one moved. Then the thief was sprinting
for the exit, all thought of money abandoned. He didn't make it.
The cop took him out with a flying tackle that carried them both
over a divider, sailing across the assistant manager's desk and
slamming onto the children's table, which collapsed to drop them
two more feet to the floor. On his back and out cold, the crimi-
nal had, by all appearances, drifted off during an early chapter   **{154}**
of *The Cat In The Hat*, which lay open beneath him.

   The customers began to chatter and stir while Grover walked
dazedly the width of the lobby. The ringing in his ears was
reminiscent of another day long gone, except that this time he
recognized the tune: it was the song of survival. He continued
on past the plain clothes detective who was busy handcuffing his
charge, and out through the heavy glass doors onto the sun-
drenched sidewalk. Once there, he paused to take in great lung-
fuls of oxygen, his heart still thumping wildly in his chest.

   Epiphany had come like a scrolling marquee as he'd lain with
his chest to the cold stone floor. God was not out to get him at
all, and after he'd gleaned that insight, it seemed funny he had
ever believed otherwise. The truth, of course, was quite the
reverse: he was *protected*. By what or by whom he had no idea,
but the invisible shield was around him constantly, and always
had been. And it was powerful. Powerful enough to keep every
conceivable threat and calamity safely at bay. Which naturally

begged the question of…*why?* Grappling with this conundrum, his gaze floated across the busy avenue to see, arising from behind the cover of a parked car opposite, a trio of concerned spectators. Two of them were little girls–twins, he could tell that even from this distance–long haired, cherubic blondes about eight years old. The other one was their mother, a woman whom he had seen before. He had seen her first at the amusement park all those years ago and repeatedly thereafter, sometimes across a roadway like this one, or through the window of a village shop, or swept along in a tide of pedestrians but always, always fixated upon him when their eyes met as he would be upon her, feeling the connection there between them, ethereal as the warming sunshine and yet every bit as essential and pure. She looked at him that way now and he smiled back at her, because suddenly, it made total sense.

"He's alright!" Grover cried, but then, fearing they couldn't hear him for the traffic noise, he added a hearty thumbs-up sign as well. At this, the mommy revealed an exuberant grin, and gestured the same signal in return. They had been waiting for their daddy and husband to come out of the bank–a customer like himself–that ruddy-faced gent in the dark blue blazer. Well, Daddy would be coming home tonight just like he was supposed to do, home to his two little angels and his adoring wife. Thanks to *him*. The maxim claimed that all roads lead to Rome, but Grover knew for certain that all his roads had led *here*. To this day, to this bank, to this minute. His eyes filled now as everything changed, as his very perception of himself was yanked out of the ground by the roots, turned topsy-turvy and repotted as fabulous topiary. He wasn't any sinner or freak or misfit! Good gracious...he was a *superhero!*

And it left him then, whatever it was, left him like a thought escapes the mind, and when he stepped from the curb in front of that truck he was still beaming back grandly at his fan club across the street, and they were calling out to him, and life was good and whole and topped with a cherry, and everyone would say later that he never felt a thing.

{156}

TiM CARTER

Episode

Big God takes up too much space, now.
He cannot play with children because he cannot
see his feet. That's real pedagogy. He might crush them
when he heaves himself sideways to itch. So he lies still. He sits
with his ass in a lake-crater letting the seasons ruin. Children cry
and call it prayer. They stay upstairs. They comb
their hair, paint dolls, and hide. He thinks sometimes that he
should quit and die, but they won't let him leave. They just want him clean.
Do you miss your wife? Do you love
your tough hands and drunk trembling fingers? Look into your
children's eyes and tell me why you had to bury her.

{157}

TIM CARTER
Massagcre

Don't forget that wolves have been killing sheep for thousands of
years; we just don't see them anymore. Cunning has grown into fine
bloody sport jackets for their shoulders.

It is March and there is a caramelized moon out. The wolves they
creep with their monocles through berry-globbed thickets, gather-
ing appetizers. A budding stench of fear, and folded napkins.

In the morning there is evidence of running and scrabble. And
blood. There are many less sheep. Wolves whistle into town in
their Cadillacs, their grins stained. Lads get new wool caps; the
girlies: mittens. Women are massaged and some wine is popped. {158}
Even the collies nap under soft thick blankets.

The honest townsfolk, though hyperopic, go desperately to detec-
tives, and wail for missing sheep. The detective paws the ground,
is still stuffed, and picks fluff from its nails. Nothing ever
turns up.

TiM CARTER
Seaglass

I remember making up the memory of you
teaching me how to swim in Rockwell Bay.
You held my armpits while I kicked up a white froth, and later
we waded through cooler shallows looking for seaglass.
They lay strewn like diamonds and I held one
in my hand. It was green
and sharp like a lie.

{159}

TIM LEACH
Little Lead Omens

Fingers of joyful boys at Christmas rip wrap
crisp as full dress uniforms from boxed squads
of little lead soldiers.

Plucked from dye-cut cardboard foxholes, sangfroid
troops, molded to heroic poses, always win
toy wars boys wage without loss.

Years later, little lead fingers rip open
gifted boys grown to soldier on in real war-
action figures out of it.

Each lies at attention, aware too late
who pays the price of toy wars turning true.
Tagged, bagged, boxed, and sent by air

freight home, with superior officer's
thank-you note, remains are flagged, churched
and hearsed in parade-dress send-off.

Bunched blooms, cut short, burst, color
grenades against grey, spews shrapnel of heavenly
scent to mask the smell of blood

from human sacrifice. Then, pay-back:
purple heart for his that failed; silver star for his
unlucky one, ribbons for tying

loose ends—grief, anger, guilt, love and loss.
Firing squads unload on forever spacious sky.
Bugle blows, gone the son, box lowers;

wrap saved, holy laundry, folded by squared
moves, given mom, giver of toy soldiers, getting
back now tri-corn pillow, symbol of blood, bone

& star-stitched bruise. Presented flag by wind-up troop
in dress-blues, she takes the wrap from white gloves
that leave no fingerprints.

{161}

TIM LEACH
Dorothy's Signature

At the bank they know she's alive by the monthly trickle
of checks she signs on dotted lines she doesn't see
without my finger pointing where.

For years she penned her name, fingers poised,
to express identity with the fluid momentum of
Vivaldi's 'Four Seasons' voiced by her violin.

Now she mouths her letters as slowly as the crawl
of her scrawl. Her thread unraveling nonetheless
authenticates her worth to Blue Cross, the IRS,

and a hairdresser. She starts at the top of the *"D"*
with a curlicue, a simulation of the over-sized bow
that topped her face, age eight, on the day

the camera caught her too-serious eyes.
Locked behind a gold-framed pane, today her
young eyes gaze across a mahogany coffee table

as if they saw this decrepit future at the end
of the line. The D's belly swells beneath the rolling
ballpoint as if bloated by hours of daytime TV

that fogged eyes see from an easy chair. Her nearly
blind eyes peer down curiously as the *"O-R-O"*
 unwinds in slow motion, as if all the time in the world

lay blank before her. Lost after the *"T-H"*, she asks
where she is. I tell her. She repeats the *"T-H"* and grins
Her déjà vu grin as if she knew, then bears down

on her thread of thought with a *"Y"* that over-rides
her magnetic code. By the time breasts swell from the *"B"*
for "Black", her maiden name, she nears the edge.

Indulging in the tight-lipped impunity of age, she presses on;
guided by the blue-lined map, the back of her hand,
down a blood-line's thinning road.

{163}

AUTHOR BIOS

ACE BOGGESS currently is incarcerated in the West Virginia correctional system. His poetry has appeared in Harvard Review, Notre Dame Review, Poetry East, RATTLE, Atlanta Review, Southeast Review, Florida Review and other journals. His books include The Beautiful Girl Whose Wish Was Not Fulfilled (poetry, Highwire Press, 2003), Displaced Hours (novel, Gatto Publishing, 2004), and, as editor, Wild Sweet Notes II, an anthology of West Virginia poetry published in 2004.

ANDREW OERKE was a Peace Corps Director in Africa and the Caribbean, and for many years president of a private and voluntary organization, working in and visiting more than 160 countries. Mr. Oerke was the recipient of a Fulbright scholarship at the Freie Universität in Berlin. His work has appeared frequently in The New Yorker, The New Republic, Poetry, and in many other publications in the U.S., England, France, Germany, Lebanon, Malawi, Kenya, the Philippines, Jamaica, and Mexico. In 2003, he was given the award for literature by the UN Society of Writers and Artists.

{164}

ARTHUR GOTTLIEB is an Oregon poet whose work has appeared in many small literary magazines, including The Ledge, Chiron Review, The Alembic, The Pacific Review, Lullwater Review & many others.

BARRY W. NORTH is a sixty-five year old recently retired refrigeration mechanic. He worked in that capacity for the local school system for twenty-eight years. Since his retirement in 2007, his poems and stories have appeared in, or are scheduled to appear in, Slipstream, Art Times, The Louisiana Review, Aries, Ginosko, and many others. His short story, "Along the Highway," has won the 2010 A.E. Coppard Prize for fiction.

BRIAN STEEN resides in Mesa, Arizona with his wife Shirley, an R.N. Brian was born in Michigan and raised in the suburbs just outside Detroit. For the past twenty years Brian has worked as a counselor with seriously mentally ill adults. Prior to counseling as a profession, Brian was an English teacher in Michigan, North Dakota and California. Brian recently completed his first novel, "All Right Now…Tomorrow" which he hopes to publish soon, with a little luck. Brian and Shirley's daughter, Vanessa, is currently a dietician in Loma Linda, California.

BROCK MARIE MOORE was viciously attacked by her muse (a life-long stalker) in the summer of 2009, after years of quietly studying computer/library science and teaching small children. When not writing, she can often be found curled up with Poe & Yeats, Galway Kinnell's Book of Nightmares, or an EC comic book.

{165}

CLARA MAE BARNHART will be graduating from Champlain College in December of 2010 with a degree in professional writing. Her favorite word is falafel, even though she has never tried one, and her favorite color is red. She hopes to keep learning as much as she can for the rest of her life in new places.

DAVID LAWRENCE has been published over five hundred times in magazines such as North American Review, Poet Lore, Slipstream, Atlanta Review, The South Carolina Review, etc. His book, Lane Changes, was published in 2007.

DAVID WRITE is a writing professor in the Central New York area and the Coordinating Editing for the journal Poet's Ink Review. David has been published in Cider Press Review, miller's pond, Aries, and Coal Hill Review, among others.

EMMA MARIE DEVINE originally from the beautiful downtown of southern Vermont, found family within her writing classes at Champlain College. This family encouraged her to study abroad in Dublin, Ireland in the spring of 2010. In Dublin, as well as Burlington, and in the world beyond, she finds inspiration for her writing in her constantly changing surroundings, introducing herself to who ever she can, and simply smiling everywhere.

ERICA A SI is an English language teacher at a refugee resettlement office. She has published in many magazines, including Phoebe, International Poetry, Haight Ashbery, and Ibbetson Street. She enjoys writing about her students and everyday experiences.

ERIN GLEESON is a Professional Writing major at Champlain College. Writing is not only something she endlessly loves, but something she feels she innately must do. She writes primarily poetry and creative non-fiction, but has worked with journalism and interned at New Hampshire Public Radio, studying radio journalism. When all is said and done, she would like to travel to learn, study and write about culture, as she is deeply interested in peoples' stories. Her ultimate goal is to grow into a travel writing, ethnographic documentarist who lives and breathes poetry.

{166}

Fired from Hallmark for writing meaningful greeting-card verse, **FRED YANNANTUONO** once ran twenty straight balls at pool; finished 183rd (out of about 10,000) at the 1985 U.S. Open Crossword Puzzle Tournament; won a yodeling contest in a German restaurant; was bitten by a guard dog in a tattoo parlor; survived a car crash with Sidney Lumet; Paul Newman once claimed to have known him for a long time; hasn't been arrested in 17 months.

Fred's work has appeared in 75 journals in 30 states. Work was nominated for a Pushcart Prize in 2006. His book, A BOILERMAKER FOR THE LADY *(www.nyqbooks.org/fredyannantuono)* has been banned in France, Latvia, and the Orkney Isles.

FREDRICK ZYDEK is the author of nine collections of poetry. Formerly a professor of creative writing and theology at the University of Nebraska and later at the College of Saint Mary, he is now a gentleman farmer when he isn't writing. His biography of Charles Taze Russell was just released from Winthrop Press. Hooked on Fish will be released later this year from Bag and Bone Press. He is the editor for Lone Willow Press.

GARY SILVA was born in Hayward, California, which is in the North Bay near Berkeley and Oakland. He has studied and practiced poetry writing at California State University, Fresno (M.A.), and U.C., Irvine (M.F.A.), among other venues. For the past twenty years he taught writing and literature at Napa Valley College but has recently retired. He is also serving as the Poet Laureate of Napa County until May, 2010. He has published numerous poems in magazines across the U.S.

JAN JOHNSON S short fiction has appeared in Bellowing Ark, The Amherst Review, Square Lake, Skylark, The Wascana Review, The Coe Review, The Antigonish Review, Spire Magazine, Lily Literary Review, Pinyon and Phantasmagoria. Her journalism and nonfiction have appeared in many publications, on TV and on radio. She completed her MFA in fiction at the Bennington Writing Seminars in Vermont. She lives and works in Portland, Oregon where she published one novel and currently is at work on another.

JAY BLAISDELL is the editor of www.JayBlaisdell.com, an on-line magazine that reviews award-winning fiction and film. He lived in The Netherlands for four years, and now resides in Nashville, where is writing a novel.

JILLIAN TOWNE wrote her piece as a sophomore in the Professional Writing Program at Champlain. Now a junior, Jillian enjoys working with and writing about food, and is working toward figuring out how those two forces will play out in her future career and life.

JIMMY J. PACK JR. is a part-time lecturer in writing at Penn State, Abington. He just finished his first creative nonfiction "novel" titled Dispatches to America: A Route 66 Memoir. He also runs a website of Road-Side American photography at rt66photos. com. Anyone interested in contacting him, send an email to *jimmyjpackjr1@mac.com.*

{168}

JOHN SANDOVAL has earned his daily bread as fire fighter, gold miner, painter of houses. From these occupations, and from idling about on street corners and in saloons, he has drawn his inspiration. He is presently residing in Cleveland, Ohio, where he is employed as late night desk clerk at the historical Alcazar Hotel.

A resident of Edwardsville, Illinois, **KATE DUVALL** is currently working on an associate's degree from Lewis & Clark Community College in Godfrey, Illinois, and just beginning to establish herself as a skilled craftswoman and author. Her poetry has been published in literary journals such as Write On!! Poetry Magazette, Pegasus, and Abbey. Her poem "The Twenty-third Psalm for Rock 'n' Roll Junkies" was inspired by her own lifelong love of rock 'n' roll and religion studies and a Dear Abby column featuring a 23rd Psalm parody encouraging people to eat healthy diets.

Literary and Fine Art Magazine of Champlain College

KATHERINE AYARS is currently earning her MFA in Creative Writing. Her work has appeared in The Raven Chronicles and So to Speak, among others. She spends her spare time sculpting neon and is endlessly in love with her boyfriend Charlie.

KEN DiMAGGIO teaches English Composition & Film Study at Capital Community College in Hartford. Besides teaching, writing, and reading, he sometimes travels and this past summer, he visited the West African country of Benin where he explored the country's traditions of Voodoo, and even met the Head Voodoo priest who said he had been expecting my visit.

MARGARET (MAGGIE) DELGUERCIO lives in Elberon, NJ. She is Associate Professor of English at Monmouth University where she teaches Shakespeare and Creative Writing. For over twenty years her work has appeared in small press journals including EDGZ, The GW review, Rhino, The Rockford Review, Ship of Fools and Sulphur River Literary Review.

MADDY HOPPERS was born in Sacramento CA on April 1, 1988. Her full name, Mary-Madeleine Noelle Hoppers means; to be born (Noelle) a tower of strength (Madeleine) in a sea of bitterness and sorrow (Mary) in a fort on a swamp (Hoppers). Maddy currently lives and works in VT with her 90-pound mutt and is constantly trying to live up to the absurd beauty of her name.

MATT McCAWLEY lives on the beach in North Carolina, works in a seafood restaurant with the international champion chowder, and fishes every other second he has.

{169}

MATT REEVY was born and resides in Portland, Maine, where he spends his time actively campaigning for indentured servitude, free market shoplifting, and repealing the 19th Amendment. His furniture fetish remains unresolved.

As a graphic designer, illustrator and writer and tons of ideas come to **MARK GONZALEZ** all the time. He is constantly working on ideas for short stories and poetry, as well as art work. For Mark, art and writing are ways to reach others, create something that lives and seemingly continues on its own. Three favorite novels of his are Slaughter House Five, Hard Boiled Wonderland and the End of the World, and Edenborn.

Previously, **MICHAEL FULOP** has had poems published in Cream City Review, Green Mountains Review, LIT, Potomac Review, and Xavier Review. He works as a psychiatrist, and lives slightly north of Baltimore City with his wife and two children.

{170}

MICHAEL S. MORRIS was born in Waterbury, CT and has lived in Sonoma, CA for 28 years. His work has appeared in over 55 literary journals, littles, and anthologies. Michael is an award winning writer and the author of two novels, one book of short stories, and nine collections of poetry. In 2007 Happy Rock Publications published his collection of poetry "A Juke Joint Played In." In 2008 Minotaur Press published "A Wink Centuries Old," as a chapbook and has agreed to publish an upcoming collection entitled "Tales from Bohemia."

PATIENCE HULBURT-LAWTON is a junior Professional Writing Major at Champlain College. She is a singer/songwriter, soon to be releasing a CD of original songs. She applies her study of writing to her lyrics and her love of poetry. *Patience is also the winner of the 2010 Willard and Maple Poetry Award.*

PETER LUDWIN is the recipient of a Literary Fellowship from Artist Trust. He was the 2007-2008 Second Prize Winner of the Anna Davidson Rosenberg Awards for poems on the Jewish experience, and was a finalist for the Muriel Craft Bailey Memorial Award. An avid traveler, for the past seven years he has been a participant in the San Miguel Poetry Week in San Miguel de Allende, Mexico. He owns a small trailer and twenty acres of land near Big Bend National Park in Texas, but lives most of the year tucked up against the Green River in Kent, Washington.

RACHEL PALMATEER has emerged from the woods of upstate New York to light Champlain College on fire. Racing across the country to jump feet first and grinning into her junior year of higher education, she will be attending Naropa University in Boulder, Colorado. She enjoys adventures and tofu with her spunky grey cat, Loki.

{171}

RANDALL BROWN teaches at and directs Rosemont College's MFA in Writing Program. He is the author of the award-winning collection Mad to Live (Flume Press, 2008) and his essay on (very) short fiction appears in The Rose Metal Press Field Guide to Writing Flash Fiction: Tips from Editors, Teachers, and Writers in the Field (Rose Metal Press, 2009). He has been published widely, both in print and online.

RICHARD LUFTIG is a retired professor of Educational Psychology and Special Education at Miami University in Ohio. He is a recipient of the Cincinnati Post-Corbett Foundation Award for Literature and a semi finalist for the Emily Dickinson Society Award. His poems have appeared in numerous literary journals in the United States and internationally in Japan, Canada, Australia, Finland, Bulgaria, Thailand, England and Hong Kong. His third chapbook was published by Dos Madres Press.

SKYLER LENDWAY is native of Nantucket Island, Massachusetts. Now a Professional Writing Major at Champlain College, Skyler enjoys immersing himself in both the college experience and the Burlington culture. Having taken classes in everything from Journalism to Nature Writing, Skyler especially enjoys writing fiction and poetry. In his free time, he enjoys playing frisbee, listening to music, enjoying a good cup of tea, playing table-top games with friends, and wandering in new places. He hopes to travel to Dublin this coming spring for a semester abroad, and expand what he believes to be a limited perspective of the world.

{172}

A retired art teacher, **STEVE BENSON** is married with three children. He and his brother recently saw published "Schooled Lives: Poems By Two Brothers," which is available on amazon.com. The Tennyson brothers in 1827 did the same thing, so the Bensons are in good company. Steve had twenty poems taken by The Christian Science Monitor, plus other poems in North American Review, Hollins Critic, Poet Lore, The Spoon River Poetry Review, MARGIE, The Briar Cliff Review, Quercus Review, Nerve
Cowboy and others.

N.Y.C.'s **SUSAN MAURER** has had eight little books published and her full-length PERFECT DARK, has been published by Ungovernable Press out of Sweden. She has had four Pushcart nominations and been published in fifteen countries.

SUSANNA RICH is a 2009 Emmy Award nominee for her poetry in Cobb Field: A Day at the Ballpark, and author of two Finishing Line Press chapbooks–Television Daddy and The Drive Home. She tours both titles as staged, audience-interactive, poetry readings directed by Ernest Wiggins. ashes, ashes: A Poet Responds to the Shoah is scheduled to open in April 2011. Susanna is Professor and Distinguished Teacher at Kean University. Please visit her at www.susannarich.com.

TIM CARTER is a sophomore at Hobart & William Smith Colleges in Geneva, New York, where he is working hard to become a high school English teacher so that he can make millions of dollars and retire early. He also once had an out-of-body experience while listening to a recording of Alan Ginsberg's "Howl". During the summer he is a student mentor at Champlain College's Young Vermont Writers' Conference. Tim was born and locally grown in Burlington, Vermont.

A 2009 Pushcart Prize nominee, **TIM LEACH** won the 2009 Russell Grant Poetry Award from University of Missouri–St. Louis MFA program. A finalist in recent River Styx, New Letters and New Millennium competitions, his poems will have soon appeared in 20 journals including: Southern Poetry Journal, Atlanta Review, New York Quarterly, Potomac Review and Sou'wester. Leach was a journalist, advertising and PR writer for forty years. A Vietnam vet, he lives in St. Louis, where he has also been a showboat actor and a recycling artist whose work has appeared in juried shows.

T. M. BEMIS is a writer and nuclear chemist residing in the Hudson Valley. His fiction has appeared in Bryant Literary Review, Confluence, Eureka Literary Magazine and other publications.

FINE ART

{175}

Willard & Maple XV

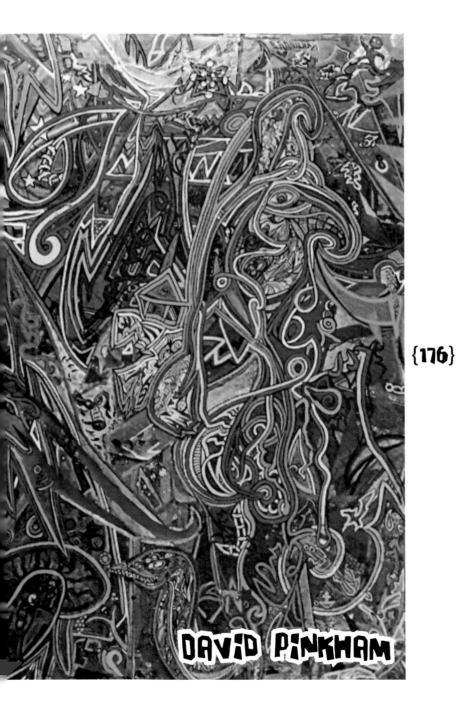

DAVID PINKHAM

{177}

{178}

JACK NICHOLS

Literary and Fine Art Magazine of Champlain College

Willard & Maple XV

PRIVATE PROPERTY
PLEASE
No Skateboarding
No Rollerblading
No Bicycling

{180}

JOHN BROWN

Literary and Fine Art Magazine of Champlain College

{181}

KYLE KELLY

Willard & Maple XV

LUCY HYDE

Literary and Fine Art Magazine of Champlain College

Willard & Maple XV

{186}

MAXENCE MASSON

Literary and Fine Art Magazine of Champlain College

{187}

MIKE SCATURO

Literary and Fine Art Magazine of Champlain College

NICK STEFANI

NICK STEFANI

PETER BARRY

Literary and Fine Art Magazine of Champlain College

SAMANTHA LAM

Literary and Fine Art Magazine of Champlain College

{196}

SARA FOWLER

Scott Moretto

Literary and Fine Art Magazine of Champlain College

{199}

{200}

STACEY KILPATRICK

Literary and Fine Art Magazine of Champlain College

{201}

{202}

TAMMY JENNINGS

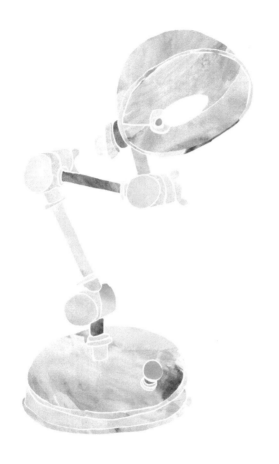

{204}

TOMMY SHIMKO